THE CATAFIGHTERS
and Merchant Aircraft Carriers

Other Books By Kenneth Poolman

THE KELLY
FAITH, HOPE & CHARITY
ILLUSTRIOUS
ARK ROYAL
ZEPPELINS OVER ENGLAND
GUNS OFF CAPE ANN
FLYING BOAT

Fiction

TEACH 'EM TO DIE
THE GIANT KILLERS
WOLF PACK

THE CATAFIGHTERS
and Merchant Aircraft Carriers

KENNETH POOLMAN

WILLIAM KIMBER · LONDON

First published in 1970 by
WILLIAM KIMBER & CO. LIMITED
22A Queen Anne's Gate, London, S.W.1

SBN 7183 0052 1

© Kenneth Poolman, 1970

Printed in Great Britain by W. & J. Mackay & Co Ltd, Chatham

Contents and Illustrations

Unless otherwise stated, all the illustrations listed below are reproduced by courtesy of the Imperial War Museum.

8 THE CATAFIGHTERS

Acknowledgments

I should like to thank all the people who have generously given their time and interest to the preparation of this book, particularly Geoffrey Banks, Lord Kilbracken, Captain E. J. Goodchild, OBE, and Terence Longdon.

I also wish to thank the Royal Air Force Historical Section, the Director of Public Relations (Navy), the Library and Photographic Section of the Imperial War Museum, and Richard Pryde and Peter Whyman of Lloyds Register for their great help in the gathering of material.

To the memory of
FLYING OFFICER J. B. KENDAL

Prologue

On April 9th, 1940, the Twilight War finally ended and the real war began. Hitler made his next move in the conquest of Europe.

The Germans marched unopposed into Denmark, and invaded Norway, which resisted them. Britain sent troops to Norway. A small force of Royal Air Force Hurricanes and Gladiators struggled against the greatly superior strength of the Luftwaffe, side by side with Fleet Air Arm fighters from carriers off the coast. Naval dive-bombers from the carriers and from the Orkneys attacked German shipping.

On May 10th the Germans invaded France, Belgium and Holland. By May 25th all Allied forces had been driven out of central Norway and the remnant of the British army in France was on the beaches of Dunkirk. Air Chief Marshal Sir Hugh Dowding, head of Fighter Command of the RAF, who had persuaded a reluctant Churchill to hold back enough of the dwindling stock of RAF Hurricanes and Spitfires from France to provide a bare minimum with which to defend Britain itself, was forced to use up more of them to give cover to the troops on the exposed beaches and the mixed armada of destroyers, paddle steamers, pleasure cruisers and yachts which had been hastily collected to bring them off. 'Fighter patrols' were flown over Dunkirk by Swordfish biplanes of the Fleet Air Arm. In the final evacuation from Norway, the *Glorious* achieved the impossible by safely embarking a RAF Hurricane squadron, which landed aboard without deck-landing hooks or previous deck-landing experience, thus paving the way for the conversion of modern fighters for carrier work. Tragically, the *Glorious* was afterwards sunk by the *Scharnhorst* and *Gneisenau*.

By June 22nd France was beaten. The move was complete. The Germans would now hold the entire western coast of Europe, from the northern tip of Norway to the Spanish border. Within the grip of this vast pincer lay Britain.

Focke-Wulf Condor 200C-1

Within easy range of coastal based German bombers, battleships and U-boats were her southern ports and the great stream of ships which used them.

Britain dug in and looked to the Navy and the RAF to keep Hitler out. Dowding hoarded his thin blue line of fighters. Everyone waited for the massed air fleets, the screeching Stukas that had blasted Rotterdam, the rumble of Panzers in English lanes. Churchill spoke to the nation of 'fighting on the beaches'.

But Rotterdam was one thing, London another. Britain had no army, but there was still the RAF, and there was always the Navy. Besides, the Panzers had just fought a great campaign on three fronts. They were not ready for Britain. And first must come the air blitz. It would take time to move the necessary strength from Germany and Norway to the French coastal airfields.

There was no definite invasion planned. It was not Hitler's, it was not the Nazi style, not while there was a Royal Navy in the Channel and a Royal Air Force still in being. Hitler's first instinct was to patch up a peace. The take-over would come later, after the softening-up by propaganda and infiltration. Through diplomatic channels the British Government encouraged this hope, to gain time.

But July came and the British were still prevaricating. Hitler decided to give them a jolt. He ordered his Luftwaffe units on the French coast to sweep the Channel of British ships and the air above it of British fighters.

The German bombers caused serious losses to Allied merchantmen and destroyers and bombed Portland and Portsmouth. The destroyers were stopped from using Dover at all and could only sail from Portsmouth at night. The Channel was closed to all ocean-going convoys, which were re-routed to west coast ports or through the North Sea round Scotland. Finally, all coastal convoys were stopped.

On July 19th Hitler appealed to the British Government to talk peace. He got no reply. Finally he lost patience. On August 1st he ordered the Luftwaffe to destroy the RAF, in the air and on the ground. Invasion barges were ordered up to the French Channel ports in preparation for Operation 'Sealion', the invasion of Britain.

By September 15th it was all over. Dowding's fiercely preserved Few had beaten down the might of the Luftwaffe and let the hot air out of Goering. Once again members of the Fleet Air Arm joined in to help the hard-pressed pilots of Fighter Command. Two courses, about forty pilots, under training at the RN Fighter School at HMS *Raven* at Yeovilton in Somerset volunteered for temporary service with the RAF.

With the invasion abandoned, the Germans fell back on the slower, less spectacular approach—the destruction of Britain's industry and morale by night bombing, and of her shipping lifeline by bombers, which had already proved their worth against ships in the Channel, by U-boats, which had almost succeeded in starving Britain in World War I, and by surface warships.

I

At the end of June, 1940, immediately after the collapse of France, the twelve four-engined Focke-Wulf 200C-1 Condors of *1 Staffel, II Gruppe, Kampfgeschwader 40*, flew into the French air base at Bordeaux-Merignac on the Bay of Biscay, led by their commanding officer, Oberst-Leutnant Edgar Peterson. They were to be attached to *IV Fliegercorps* under *Luftflotte 3* for operations in support of attacks on the British Isles.

Peterson had himself formed the first *staffel* of long-range maritime reconnaissance-bombers at Bremen on October 1st, 1939, using six machines built originally for the Imperial Japanese Navy and six standard FW 200 Luftwaffe transports, all adapted from the successful twenty-six-seat FW airliner. Before they flew to Bordeaux-Merignac *1 Staffel* had been re-equipped from 200C-0's, and the C-1's were new machines.

There were some changes in gun armament from the 200C-0. The 7.9-millimetre upper forward-firing machine-gun immediately abaft the cockpit was now housed in a flexible mounting inside a fixed raised cupola instead of a hydraulically operated turret. The after upper 7.9-millimetre machine-gun on a flexible mounting remained the same, but in place of the third machine-gun firing aft and downward through a belly hatch, the 200C-1 incorporated a large blister, or 'gondola', on the underside, offset to starboard with one Oerlikon-type cannon on a flexible mounting firing forward and one 7.9-millimetre machine-gun firing aft. The crew of five comprised pilot, co-pilot, a navigator who quadrupled as bombardier, radio-operator and gunner, an engineer who doubled as a gunner, and a rear gunner.

The FW 200C-1 Condors carried four 551-pounder bombs (two on racks on the extended nacelles of the outboard engines, two on racks outboard of the engines), with a rack for a fifth in the gondola, though this one was sometimes a cement bomb used to check the accuracy of the rather primitive Revi bomb-sight.

With their range of 2,000 miles the new Condors could reach out into the Atlantic well beyond the range of any aircraft based in the British Isles.

This made them especially useful when the British Admiralty closed all southern ports in Britain to heavy shipping and switched it all north to the Clyde and the Mersey, re-routing ships as far out in the Atlantic as possible to escape the Luftwaffe and the German Navy. But they could not escape the U-boats or the Condors.

Hitler had concentrated on surface warships, which he intended to use as hit-and-run raiders against Allied convoys, as they were too few to face the Home Fleet in battle. As a result of this U-boat production was not geared to major attack when France fell. Admiral Doenitz could put only ten submarines out on the convoy lanes to start with.

Above the water the Condors swooped into action like giant birds of prey. They took off from Bordeaux-Merignac, and flew a wide arc round the Atlantic coast of Eire looking for 'targets of opportunity'.

There were plenty of these. Over 2,000,000 tons of shipping were being turned round at British ports each month. Most of the ships sailed in convoy, but, alone or in convoy, they had hardly any air defence at all, only the inadequate anti-aircraft guns of the very small number of escort vessels which could be spared.

Peterson's Condors were able to go in at masthead height. They had no proper bombsights for low-level attacks, but would drop all their 551-pounders in a stick on a ship. At least one of the bombs would find its target. In August and September of 1940 they sank more than 90,000 tons.

The Admiralty took some steps to counter them. Convoys were routed further

RN Fighter Catapult Ship Springbank

west, though this widened the gap between air cover from Gibraltar and by Coastal Command of the RAF in Britain. Luftwaffe bases in France were bombed. Coastal Command's strength in Northern Ireland was increased from fifty-six to ninety-six aircraft. Guns were borrowed from shore defences and given to the merchantmen. Only a few were lucky enough to get 20-millimetre Oerlikon cannon. Most ships had to make do with World War I 4-inch or Lewis light (.303-inch) machine-guns, and there were not even enough of these to go round.

Other countermeasures were more ingenious than effective. They included the Holman Projector, or 'Spud Gun', which fired Mills hand grenades, the parachute and cable device, in which a rocket carried a wire line upwards and released a parachute to suspend the wire in front of an enemy aircraft, and the false 'straggler' which lagged behind a convoy, packed with hidden guns in the manner of the World War I Q-ships to trap the unwary Condor.

The Chief of Air Staff had no confidence in these measures. He was, he told his colleagues on the Chiefs of Staff Committee, '. . . convinced that neither shore-based aircraft . . . nor gun armament can secure our shipping . . . against the scale and type of attack that we must now expect . . . The only method of protection likely to be effective is the ship-borne high performance fighter . . .'

It was no use looking to the Navy for these. Their few precious aircraft carriers were all heavily committed to use with the Battle Fleet at Gibraltar or in the Mediterranean, where the convoys to Malta and Alexandria were crucial. The 'high performance fighters' would have to operate, said the Chief of Air Staff, 'from specially converted ships which must accompany each convoy'.

The Royal Naval Director of Air Material, Captain M. S. Slattery, put forward two ways of providing fighter protection for convoys at sea. He proposed 'The fitting of catapults to suitable merchant ships' and 'The fitting of the simplest possible flight decks and landing equipment to suitable merchant ships'. With regard to the latter he suggested that 'the merchant ship carrier, a feature of which would be the continuance of its ability to carry its normal cargo, should be investigated at once'. His proposals contained a general plan for operating six Hurricanes from a converted merchantman, with arrester wires and a safety barrier, but with no lifts or hangars.

On October 26th, 1940, Hauptmann Jope's Condor crew sighted the Canadian Pacific liner *Empress of Britain*, a famous and beautiful ship and a symbol of the pre-war power of the British Mercantile Marine, in position

Fairey Fulmar landing on a carrier. The arrester hook has caught the first wire

54°33′ North, 10°49′ West, seventy miles north-west of Donegal Bay, on her way home from the Middle East.

Jope's attack left her crippled and on fire. Two days later, dragging along under tow, she had reached 55°16′ North, 09°50′ West, when she was picked up by the periscope of *U-32*, commanded by Hans Jenish, a U-boat ace with over 100,000 tons of Allied shipping already to his credit. The great liner sank four minutes after Jenish's torpedoes struck her.

In October the Directorate of Research and Development (Air) asked Hawkers if Hurricane Mark I's could be modified for catapult work. They were told that a prototype could be completed in five weeks.

On January 19th, 1941, the Admiralty ordered twenty sets of catapult spools and modification kits as specified by Hawkers. A fortnight later thirty more kits were ordered. The Battle of the Atlantic Committee was informed and told that catapult equipment had been ordered for fifty merchantmen and that a start had been made in selecting the ships to be fitted. Work was begun on thirty-five merchant ships, ranging from 2,500 to 12,000 tons, at Liverpool, Bristol, Cardiff and Clydeside.

These vessels would be called Catapult Aircraft Merchant Ships, which was soon conveniently abbreviated to CAM-ships. They would continue to carry their normal cargoes and fly the Red Ensign, have all-Merchant Navy crews, except for a few Royal Navy gunners, and always remain part of the convoy. Pilots for their aircraft would be drawn at first from Fleet Air Arm officers with previous experience in catapult spotting aircraft of the Fleet, but the remainder, the majority of the men needed to fly and maintain the 'Catafighters', were to come from Fighter Command of the Royal Air Force.

Some early CAM-ships carried a two-seat naval Fulmar fighter each, but for the majority fifty Hurricane I's were acquired for conversion into Sea Hurricanes, and the work carried out by Folland Aircraft at Hamble, in Hampshire. Catapult spools were fitted and the airframes were strengthened to withstand the extra stresses set up by catapulting. These fifty land Hurricanes, many of them veterans of the Battle of Britain, were re-designated Sea Hurricane IA's.

To supplement the CAM-ships the Admiralty also selected four ships, the Armed Merchant Cruisers *Ariguani*, *Maplin* and *Springbank*, which had been in use as Ocean Boarding Vessels, and the old naval seaplane-carrier *Pegasus*, to be equipped with a catapult each and a Fulmar or a Sea Hurricane.

These vessels were officially called Fighter Catapult Ships. The three ex-Armed Merchant Cruisers retained their guns and their ships' companies, who were mostly Merchant Navy men serving under the special T124X articles, and were commanded by ex-Merchant Navy captains of the Royal Navy Reserve. Aircrew and maintenance personnel for the aircraft would come from the Fleet Air Arm. The Fighter Catapult Ships did not carry cargo, and would work as part of the convoy escort, flying the White Ensign.

Captain Slattery's second proposal was also taken up. The Norddeutscher Lloyd Line's 8,000 ton *Hannover*, which had carried fruit from the West Indies before the war, had been caught off St. Domingo trying to creep home through the blockade by the cruiser *Dunedin* and the destroyer *Assiniboine* and eventually brought to Britain. She was put into dockyard hands for conversion into a small aircraft carrier.

Meanwhile the sinkings went on. Between August 1st, 1940, and February 9th, 1941, the Condors from Bordeaux-Merignac sank eighty-five Allied ships, a total of 363,000 tons. Winston Churchill called them 'The Scourge of the Atlantic'.

The FW 200C-1 was now being replaced by the C-2, with the airframe, which had proved unequal to the shocks and strains of combat flying, partially strengthened. By March, 1941, Peterson's unit had been increased to a full three-*staffel gruppe*, with thirty-six machines.

In April the four Fighter Catapult Ships were ready for sea. Two were put on the Gibraltar run, two on the North American route to Halifax, Nova Scotia.

2

Four fighter aircraft and a collection of old 4-inch and Lewis guns were not going to stop the 'Scourge of the Atlantic', but on the 5th of May, 1941, the Merchant Ship Fighter Unit of the Royal Air Force was formed at Speke Airport, Liverpool, 'to implement the policy of providing merchant shipborne fighter aircraft for the protection of shipping against air attack'.

In this way the RAF was to reciprocate for the help given to them by the Fleet Air Arm Swordfish, Skuas and Rocs over Dunkirk and the naval Hurricane and Spitfire pilots in the Battle of Britain. It was an outstanding example of the way in which the Senior and Junior Services co-operated in the interests of the war effort, a lesson which the Germans never learned.

Commanding Officer of the new unit was Wing Commander E. S. Moulton-Barrett. On the 9th the first pilot, Pilot Officer H. J. Davidson, reported for duty, and two days later the airmen personnel began reporting. On the 12th four Hurricanes arrived from Yeovilton, and the veteran pilot Squadron Leader Louis Strange, DSO, MC, DFC and bar, reported as Squadron Leader, Flying Duties. During the next few days more pilots arrived, some from catapult and Hurricane conversion courses at Debden and Farnborough.

RAF pilots were not normally called upon to be fired from a catapult. Even Squadron Leader Strange found the experience bizarre and a little frightening when he tried it out.

Sitting tightly strapped in the cockpit of the fighter straddling its take-off trolley at the after end of the catapult, he opened the throttle right out to maximum revs. The aircraft shook and vibrated under him. He pushed his head back hard against the head-rest, raised his right hand and chopped it briskly down. For a second he thought the rockets had misfired. Then there was a bang, only just audible above the roaring racket of the engine, and a diffused flash from beneath the aircraft. Contrary to what he had expected, there was no jolt at all, only a hard shove of his body against the back of the seat.

The aircraft hurtled on its trolley along the rails of the catapult. 'In that rush down the runway,' Strange reported, 'I realised everything but was powerless to act until automatically I found myself quite normally at the controls, in the air, nursing the machine for more feel and airspeed. The weather was good, the wind calm.'

On a subsequent launch one rocket in the cluster failed to fire, with the result that the aircraft went off the catapult at slightly reduced speed. Strange was unaware of the rocket failure, but felt the wheels touch the ground lightly as he left the catapult. He knew that this was normal for some launches, and had plenty of speed in hand by then. He kept straight and level for a little longer than usual, then did a rapid climbing turn. He established that with the use of 30° flap and $6\frac{1}{4}$ pounds boost a perfect take-off could be made without any loss of height at all. In many cases the aircraft climbed directly off the trolley when the airspeed was well over 80 mph.

The catapult launches were part of a very condensed pre-operational course which lasted a fortnight. Included on these courses were Fighter Direction Officers, one of which would be carried in each CAM-ship. The FDO's were all drawn from the Navy, and most of them were RNVR sub-lieutenants. It would be their job to assist their pilot to an interception by VHF (Very High Frequency) radio and sometimes with the use of radar, then known as RDF (Radio Direction Finding), and also to pass him a course to steer for the nearest land after the combat, if there was land within range of his machine. If there was no landfall within range, which was far more likely, the pilot would ditch or bale out near a convoy escort to be picked up.

After introductory lectures on the duties of the Merchant Ship Fighter Unit, pilots and fighter direction officers split up for separate lectures on their respective roles. The individual responsibilities of the pilot in a CAM-ship operation were stressed. It was pointed out that an enormous amount of time and money was being spent putting each aircraft aboard a CAM-ship, and that success finally depended solely upon him. Prior to the inclusion of CAM-ships in Atlantic convoys, losses from bombing had been frequent, and his main responsibility was to put a stop to this. There would be times when a single pilot in his Hurricane would be the only air protection a convoy had.

To be a successful CAM-ship pilot he must be keen and reliable, have tact and initiative in his relations with the Merchant Navy personnel of the ship, and

Sea Hurricane V.7246 ready for take off from the catapult of a CAM-ship,
Halifax, Nova Scotia

above all be a first-class pilot and good in combat, for he might be called upon to engage the enemy after long periods without having flown. If he and the ship's master agreed he might be given instruction and allowed to qualify as a watch-keeper on the bridge. As Commanding Officer of the RAF unit, he was responsible for their welfare. He should encourage them to study in their spare time and prepare themselves for re-mustering or re-classification, and give them assistance. Pilot and crew must always be kept fit and it was the pilot's duty to promote sport and games.

The RAF unit would sign ship's articles as members of the crew and on board ship would all be under the final jurisdiction of the master. The pilot was responsible to the master for the RAF crew and the operation of the aircraft. He had to be able to advise the master on everything affecting the operation of the machine and the conditions under which it could be used.

A pilot was told how to supervise the maintenance and protection of air-frame, engine and guns in heavy weather in the Atlantic when spray and green seas would probably drench the aircraft. Instructions as to what to do if the smell of engine room and greasy food got at the RAF crew and put *them* out of action were less explicit.

Theory was mixed with practice, which included interceptions, air-to-air firing and fighting, and solo cross-country navigation. On the ground the pilot spent much time in the Link trainer, learned to swing his compasses, practised sighting his guns, and listened to more instructions on crew administration, law and discipline. There were classes on aircraft recognition, and the details of the Focke-Wulf 200 were exhaustively studied, stressing weaknesses and blind spots. The pilot was shown how to pack his own parachute and dinghy, and had to jump into a swimming bath in full flying kit to give him practice in survival in the sea.

Then came the practice catapult launches, of which he usually did three. On May 8th a catapult arrived for use on the spot at Speke. Fighter direction exercises followed. The FDO practised controlling his pilot in the air, sometimes using RDF to pass him a course and bearing, sometimes directing him by visual signals alone.

After this the course was over and they were ready to go to a ship. A Merchant Ship Fighter Unit crew normally consisted of two officer pilots, one fitter, one rigger, one armourer, one radio telephony operator, from the RAF; a RN or RNVR fighter direction officer and a seaman torpedoman, who was in fact an electrician.

Top: *Sea Hurricane being loaded on to a training catapult on land*
Centre: *Sea Hurricane at the point of launching*
Bottom: *training catapult rocket cluster*

As selected ships became available catapults were fitted. The aircraft was loaded on a trolley fitted to a seventy-foot steel runway mounted over the fo'c'sle head of the ship on the port side. The trolley was propelled by a cluster of thirteen rockets fired electrically by the Catapult Directing Officer (CDO), who was sometimes the second pilot, sometimes a ship's officer, from a blast shelter erected beside the catapult. The aircraft would be launched only on visual sighting of an enemy aircraft on the orders of the Senior Officer, Escort, using a simple system of hand and flag signals between the pilot, Catapult Directing Officer and the ship's master.

3

The first pilot to be catapulted from a CAM-ship was Sub-Lieutenant M. A. Birrell, RN, one of the Naval pilots who had fought with the RAF in the Battle of Britain. He embarked in the *Michael E.*, the first CAM-ship to put to sea, which sailed on May 27th, 1941.

They sighted no hostile aircraft while passing through the danger zone, extending for about six hundred miles west into the Atlantic, but on the fourth day out the *Michael E.* was torpedoed and sunk by a U-boat. The survivors, including Sub-Lieutenant Birrell, were picked up after twenty hours in the boats, but the ship's Sea Hurricane was lost. Birrell's next ship was the Fighter Catapult Ship *Ariguani*, which had been requisitioned from Elders and Fyffe's Line at the outbreak of war, and had once carried bananas from the West Indies to Bristol.

The first Merchant Ship Fighter Unit trial aircraft launch from a ship was carried out from the *Empire Rainbow* at Glasgow on the last day of May, 1941, and was a failure. Another attempt on June 4th, however, succeeded. Other successful trials followed with the *Empire Moon*. Squadron Leader Moulton-Barrett personally supervised these trials and saw that everything was in order for the departure of these first two operational units. Pilot Officer Davidson embarked in the *Empire Rainbow* and Pilot Officer Campbell in the *Empire Moon*.

While *Empire Rainbow* and *Empire Moon* were at sea, two other CAM-ships were completed and sent out with the convoys. On June 8th Pilot Officer Ball joined the *Empire Spray*, and his 'Hurricat' was embarked on the 11th. On the 18th Pilot Officer Greenwood and his crew left Speke to join the *Empire Flame*, and on the 20th RAF crews embarked in the *Empire Spring* and *Empire Sun*. On the 24th Flying Officer Turner joined the *Novelist*, on the 26th Flying Officer Fisher the *Eastern City*, taking part in successful trials on the following day. On the 27th Flying Officer J. B. Kendal joined the *Empire Ocean*.

In June the conversion of the *Hannover* was completed. It was the practice to prefix the names of all merchant ships built, or re-built, during the war with 'Empire', as in World War I new ships' names all contained the word 'War'. *Hannover* was re-named *Empire Audacity*. She carried six fighters, not the Hurricanes suggested in Captain Slattery's recommendations, but American Grumman Wildcats, re-named Martlets in the Fleet Air Arm, obtained under the Lease-Lend agreement. They were slower than Hurricanes but very strong machines especially designed for the shocks of carrier landings.

These gave the *Empire Audacity* the power of six catapult ships rolled into one, with the extra advantage that her fighters had a landing deck to come back to and could be used to fly regular patrols, although compared with a Fleet carrier she was still a primitive little ship.

Her flight deck was a very short one, only 420 feet long, about half the length of the *Ark Royal*'s. Where the big carriers had six or more arrester wires, this small ship, which would be much livelier in a rough sea, had only two. She had a wire crash barrier for'ard and just aft of that one more wire. This one had a much shorter pull-out than the other two and a correspondingly fiercer retardation effect. A pilot who hooked this one could expect a bad jolt. *Audacity*'s bridge consisted of a small steel box, doubling as wheelhouse and aircraft control platform, placed for'ard level with the flight deck on the starboard side. One bad feature she had in common with the catapult ships was that her aircraft when aboard would have to remain exposed to the elements, as she had no hangar. The Martlets would need to be rugged. So would their pilots. At least they had the advantage of sleeping in the staterooms in which the *Hannover* had once accommodated a few passengers as well as her cargo of bananas. There were no bananas in *Empire Audacity*'s holds, or any other cargo. Like the Fighter Catapult Ships she was wholly a warship, an escort vessel.

Five more auxiliary carrier conversions had been started in Britain in May, 1941, and six more requested from the USA. But it would be many months before these were in service. In the meantime the air defence of Allied convoys in the mid-Atlantic gap would rest with the CAM-ships, the *Empire Audacity*'s six Martlets (when the ship had worked up to operational efficiency, which would take several weeks), and the Fighter Catapult Ships. In the year ending in June, 1941, German aircraft had sunk over a million tons of Allied and neutral shipping, although this was only a third of the tonnage sunk by U-boats. German capital ships, cruisers and E-boats had sunk another 848,000 tons, and mines had accounted for a further 300,000 tons.

The stop-gap catapult ships had had teething troubles. *Ariguani*, for example, had a bad patch with her Fulmar at sea in June, 1941. Having weighed and joined convoy OB (Outward Bound) 331 on June 9th, the high-pressure gauge of the aircraft's machine-gun firing gear was found to be defective, and the air bottle empty. The air bottle was changed for a spare and the empty one re-charged by obliging hands in the destroyer *Bulldog* when *Ariguani* reached Reykjavik in Iceland, where they also managed to scrounge a new high-pressure gauge from the RAF.

On June 14th *Ariguani* weighed and left Reykjavik to join convoy HX 130. The Fulmar was manned and the engine run up on test. On testing switches it was found that when the port magneto was switched off the engine failed altogether. The fault was traced to the starboard magneto, which was removed and tested as far as possible in the rudimentary conditions of the ship's workshop, and found unserviceable. A new spare magneto, as supplied to the ship, was fitted and tested on the engine. After this gruelling work, which went on through the night, with the ship pitching and rolling in dirty weather, the new magneto also failed. The weary mechanics removed it and stripped it down to locate the

Sea Hurricane V.6756 aboard the CAM-ship Empire Tide. *This aircraft was originally a Hurricane Mark I built in 1940 and converted to a Sea Hurricane Mark IA*

Empire Tide's *Sea Hurricane from the starboard side*

fault. They found that the lead from the condenser across the coils was not making proper contact, causing a loss of voltage. This lead was repaired and after testing the magneto was replaced in the aircraft. The engine was re-timed and run up. Full revolutions were still not reached and there was some unhealthy vibration. A recheck of the timing revealed nothing, but finally it was found that the connection inside the insulated adapter of number two cylinder in B bank was not making contact with the spark plug. Most of this work had to be done on the rolling wing of the aircraft high above the fo'c'sle head in the wind, spray and rain. The bad connection was soldered firm and the engine run up again.

Full revs were reached this time, and the pilot, eye cocked always at the clouds for Focke-Wulfs, felt less anxious. The next second his windscreen was covered and completely obscured by a jet of oil. The oil came from a leak in the pipes of the constant-speed airscrew unit. The mechanics struggled to try and stop the leak, although they knew that in these conditions it was practically hopeless. By this time, however, the convoy was inside The Minches in comparative safety, and *Ariguani* left to proceed independently to Belfast.

On land—or even in the well-equipped shelter of a carrier's hangar—the Fulmar's maladies would have been a mere nuisance. On the fo'c'sle of a catapult ship in a gale they made a nightmare for the air party. One cowling panel was blown out of the crew's hands while they were struggling to replace it.

The first CAM-ships with Merchant Ship Fighter Unit crews aboard were reporting no contacts with enemy aircraft. On July 1st Pilot Officer Varley embarked in the *Empire Gale*. On the 3rd Pilot Officer Watson joined the *Empire Dell* and Pilot Officer Fenwick the *Empire Franklyn*. Trials aboard the *Empire Dell* on the 4th were successful, and on the 6th the first rocket launch was made from Speke, with Mr. Crawfoot from the Royal Aircraft Establishment at Farnborough as Directing Officer. A successful launch was made using ten rockets. In the future MSFU pilots could make their training launches at Speke and avoid the time wasting trips to Debden or Farnborough. Throughout July trials were conducted on board the new CAM-ships *Empire Wave, Empire Eve, Empire Rowan, Helencrest, Dalton Hall, Empire Spring, Daghestan, Empire Day* and *Empire Hudson*. More CAM-ships followed as they became available for catapult conversion.

On July 19th the *Empire Rainbow*, first CAM-ship with a MSFU crew, returned from an uneventful round trip across the Atlantic, and Davidson, his crew and his Sea Hurricane were disembarked. Other CAM-ship crews returned without having seen action.

It was a Fighter Catapult Ship pilot who first attacked a Focke-Wulf Condor. On August 3rd the *Maplin* was on her way to pick up a convoy when she sighted a Focke-Wulf low on the horizon ten miles astern. Six minutes later, as the convoy came in sight, *Maplin*'s Sea Hurricane IA was launched, piloted by Lieutenant R. W. H. Everett, RNVR, a champion steeplechase rider who had won the Grand National on Gregalach in 1929.

Everett got within one and a half miles of the Focke-Wulf before it seemed to notice his presence. After chasing it for nine minutes he ranged up alongside the big machine at six hundred yards and slightly above it. When the Hurricane was slightly ahead of the Condor's starboard quarter the German's stern cannon opened fire. The shells curved away underneath or fell short of the Hurricane. The German pilot had opened the throttle. As the Hurricane struggled to draw right abeam of the bomber the Condor's forward cannon joined in. Again the fire fell underneath or short. Suddenly the Condor turned sharply to port, then immediately turned back on to its original course. Everett was now on its starboard bow, and three machine-guns as well as the forward cannon were firing on him. He did a quick turn to port and opened fire just abaft the beam, firing five-second bursts all the way until he was forty yards astern of the enemy.

Another short burst at this range and his guns were empty. He saw pieces flying off the starboard side of the Focke-Wulf, which seemed to be alight inside the fuselage. He lost sight of the enemy then as oil was splashing over his windscreen obscuring his forward view. He jumped to the conclusion that his engine oil system had been badly hit, and decided to abandon the aircraft while he still had charge of the situation. Twice he tried to bale out, but each time the aircraft nosed down and trapped him when he was half out. He changed his mind and ditched successfully near the destroyer *Wanderer*, which rapidly lowered a boat and picked him up. The oil on his windscreen had actually come from the Condor, which crashed into the sea. Nine days afterwards, on August 12th, Everett described his victory to MSFU pilots at Speke.

The catapult aircraft and increased anti-aircraft armament in the merchant ships had already put the Condor bombers off their stroke, so that they were now being used mainly for shadowing the convoys and had orders not to initiate an attack but to avoid fighters if possible. The Condor suffered from lack of armour and its fuel lines were all located in the particularly vulnerable underbelly. It had never been designed for combat, and the strain of violent manoeuvering and long ocean patrols weakened airframes, which frequently cracked up. *KG40* often had three-quarters of its strength unserviceable.

The new FW 200C-3, which began to reach *KG40* in the late summer of 1941, was a much improved machine. The weak rear spar in the wing, as well as the fuselage, had been greatly strengthened, and the C-3 had better engines, the 9-cylinder air-cooled BMW-Bramo 323R-2 Fafnirs with methanol-water injection. Potential bomb load had been increased to 4,626 pounds, comprising two 1,102-pounders, two 551-pounders and twelve 110-pounders, though for its normal offensive-reconnaissance role the Condor continued to carry only four 551-pounders. Gun armament had also been increased. The upper fixed cupola had been replaced by a low-drag Fu19 hydraulic turret with one 7.9-millimetre machine-gun, and two 7.9's placed behind sliding beam panels had been added. In the 200C-3U/1 there was a HDL 151 forward turret with one 15-millimetre MG 151 cannon instead of the Fu19 turret, and another 20-millimetre cannon replaced the machine-gun in the belly gondola. It was probably a machine of this type which was destroyed by Lieutenant Everett. The drag of the HDL turret, however, reduced the aircraft's speed by 16–18 mph, and the next mark, the 200C-3U/2, reverted to the Fu turret.

Empire Tide's *Sea Hurricane* with, left to right, *Flight Lieutenant Turley-George (senior pilot) and Flying Officer C. Fenwick (second pilot)*

The FW 200's also co-operated with submarines. When France fell U-boat production had been in low gear, but when the German invasion of Britain was cancelled it was speeded up. In the autumn of 1940 the U-boats had begun to work in 'wolf packs' to improve their chances of sighting convoys. Five or six U-boats would be stationed at intervals across the probable course of a convoy. The first boat to sight smoke or masts on the horizon would report by radio any change of course. The rest of the pack, with little to fear from the few poorly armed, unco-ordinated escorts, could use their surface speed to get ahead of the convoy and attack on the surface at night. A U-boat on the surface could make sixteen or seventeen knots, much faster than the average convoy which maintained about eight knots, and there were some special 'slow' convoys, collections of the oldest, slowest ships, which had a maximum speed of five knots.

This was where the Focke-Wulf Condor came in—it could act as contact plane for a wolf pack. On reporting a convoy, a Condor captain might be told to shadow it, while its position was passed to the Flag Officer, Submarines, at Brest, who then directed his U-boats to the target, helped by the FW shadower, which transmitted a radio direction-finding signal. The plane was not in direct touch with the submarines, but passed all information to the U-boat Headquarters, which controlled both. Allied seamen dreaded the lean grey aircraft sniffing round the horizon as the inevitable forerunner of U-boats.

On September 13th, 1941, the *Empire Audacity* sailed for Gibraltar with her first convoy, OG74. At sea the six Martlets were organised in section pairs. Two took the dawn patrol, two the dusk, with one machine flying clockwise, the other counter-clockwise round the convoy. Another pair was at Immediate Readiness on deck, two more pilots stood by in the Ready Room.

On the 15th Sub-Lieutenant Lamb, RN, and Sub-Lieutenant E. M. Brown, RNVR, were on patrol when Lamb sighted a U-boat submerging. They warned the convoy but could not do anything to damage the U-boat as they carried nothing more lethal than four 0.5-inch machine-guns. They dived on the submarine but their bullets rattled off the hull. The same two sighted another diving U-boat at dusk on the 20th, twelve miles west of the convoy.

Two ships were torpedoed and sunk that night. The rescue ship *Walmer Castle* and the salvage tug *Thames* stayed behind and were picking up survivors in the early hours of the morning when Sub-Lieutenant N. H. Patterson, RN, and Sub-Lieutenant G. R. P. Fletcher, RNVR, on dawn patrol from *Audacity*, were vectored by her Fighter Direction Officer, Lieutenant J. Parry, RNVR, an ex-Cambridge don, on to a Condor which was heading for the rescue ships.

It was a race which the Condor just won. Diving on the *Walmer Castle* the FW dropped a stick of bombs across her and set her on fire, then made for the *Thames*. At this point the two Martlets caught up with it. Patterson made a quarter attack, then Fletcher attacked from the beam with a full deflection shot. He fired only thirty-five rounds from each of his Brownings, but they found one of the FW's notorious structural weaknesses, and the whole tail unit of the Condor broke off.

4

In the autumn of 1941 convoys on the Gibraltar run were more susceptible to air attack than those on the North Atlantic and Russian routes, and the *Empire Audacity* and the Fighter Catapult Ships, all of which, as purely escort vessels, had more freedom of action than the cargo carrying CAM-ships, were reserved for the Gibraltar route from July.

CAM-ships were kept at first in the North Atlantic convoys. The MSFU crews had to surmount many difficulties. To begin with they had to get used to the motion, often very lively. At least one pilot pulled off his helmet and was sick in that rather than make the RAF a laughing stock in front of the seamen.

Routine inspection of the aircraft, perched high on its trolley on top of the catapult well for'ard, was often dangerous in bad weather. 'I did not consider it safe for the armourer to climb out on the wings, even with the protective body lines,' one pilot reported. Parts of the catapult could be slippery with grease, and it was all too easy to trip over the electrical lead from the trolley, which might wrench a wire away from one of the terminals on the plugs as well as put a key man in sick bay.

Wet and cold were of course constant obstacles to good maintenance of the aircraft. As soon as the ship put to sea a film of salty scum would begin to form on the skin of the machine, and the gun barrels would start to rust inside. Damp air would get into the gun chambers and make it very difficult to keep the gun in perfect condition for firing. It was found necessary to remove all the recoiling parts when the ship was clear of the danger zone and cover the casings with heavy grease; canvas covers had to be made for the gun barrels and covers were also needed for the rockets. Dampness caused earths in the firing circuits. Corrosion from the salt spray could put trolley wheels out of action, gun wells, breech blocks and barrels, IFF switches, sparking plugs, contact breakers and any part of the electrical system. Dope pealed off everywhere, throttles jammed.

'Very rough sea,' one report ran, 'and 65 mph gale resulted in A/C getting soaked in sea water continuously for four days. Covers were ripped off, airframe corroded, engine mags and all electrical gear setting up currents.' Rough weather could snap aircraft lashings, make bracing wires too slack or too taut, fill the fuselage with water, distort the airframe.

Living conditions varied considerably. Sometimes the airmen were given cramped accommodation, though this was often no worse than the ship's company enjoyed. There was little variety in the food, which was often noticeably worse than the RAF men would have had ashore. 'In all,' one report complained indignantly, 'the quarters and food are below the standard associated with the poorest of society . . . The food aft is bad, and the living quarters worse.' An outbreak of boils and spots among RAF crewmen was blamed on the stodgy food.

Relations with the Merchant Navy crew also varied. Harmony depended mainly on a good relationship between the senior RAF pilot and the ship's master. This was not always established. Some pilots complained of lack of

CAM-ship Empire Tide *in convoy to Murmansk*

co-operation by the captain, others of too much interference by him in purely air matters. In these cases great tact was required by the pilot. Of one particular master the pilot wrote, 'Dealing with him, studied acquiescence is better than self-assertion and will accomplish anything.' Merchant Navy men, masters included, did not always like the presence of the RAF on board their ships. Some feared that a CAM-ship would draw special attention from bombers and U-boats. For his part a young, keen pilot could be touchy, bumptious or impatient. In some cases, inevitably, pilot and master simply did not hit it off. Relations between the non-commissioned RAF ranks and the Merchant Navy crew were generally good and easily established, once the inevitable jibes at the 'Brylcreem Boys' had been aired. Over all, the MSFU crews were well received by the men who had them to thank for protection against the enemy in the sky, and were, for the most part, well aware of the debt.

On November 1st at 1505 hours the CAM-ship *Empire Foam* was in position 55°12′ North, 32°16′ West, steaming on course 022° at nine knots for home when a four-engined enemy bomber was sighted about ten miles dead ahead. Two minutes later the enemy was definitely identified as a Focke-Wulf Condor. Aboard *Empire Foam* was Number 14 MSFU crew, with a Sea Hurricane and its pilot, Flying Officer G. W. Varley, and Sub-Lieutenant H. Norman Gostelow as Fighter Direction Officer. Gostelow told the ship's Master to launch the aircraft. There was a light breeze blowing and the sea was calm, with only a slight swell. The wind was coming from dead ahead, so it was not necessary for the *Empire Foam* to alter course or to leave the convoy, when she would have been very vulnerable to any lurking U-boat.

The drill for launching was comparatively simple. When the ship was about to begin flying operations she hoisted the Aeroplane Flag ('F' flag in International Code, white with a red diamond). With the aircraft manned, the R/T link between pilot and FDO tested, and the rocket installation checked satisfactorily, the order 'Stand by to launch' passed from Master to Catapult Directing Officer by telephone was repeated directly by him to the aircraft's crew.

The alarm rattler sounded. The crew member responsible, the second pilot or an NCO, made a last quick check to see that the flight path was clear, personnel under cover. Then he removed the front locking bolt keep pins from the trolley and took them to the CDO, reporting, 'Catapult ready for firing.'

'Right.' The CDO went through his check list. Front spool holding back clamps, trolley securing bar, front locking bolt keep pins, tail securing bar—all in their proper stowages in the blast shelter. Nothing left in position to impede the aircraft. Firing switch in the OFF position. Plugs in SAFETY LINK. He positioned himself where he could see both pilot and bridge and put his finger on the switch.

A last look to see that everyone was under cover from the blast. The noise from the aircraft's engine was now so loud that he could not have trusted a telephone to make himself understood. He used a blue flag, which he now raised. The Master, on the bridge, saw the flag, understood that everything was ready for launching, and held up his own blue flag, which meant 'Launch as soon as ready'.

The pilot, watching the CDO's flag, opened his throttle wide as soon as he saw the flag rotated in the air, locked the throttle, pressed himself back against the seat and the headrest, and raised his hand in the air.

The CDO watched the rise and fall of the bows, judging the safest moment at which to send the aircraft off. Then he pressed the switch.

If everything were in working order, there was a flash and a loud bang, the aircraft shot forward down the runway and was airborne. Sometimes nothing happened. Then the CDO grabbed his red flag and waved it in the air. He hurriedly checked his gear. There might be a break in the circuit somewhere, perhaps a loose safety link or badly adjusted points. Sometimes rockets failed and the aircraft was shot humiliatingly, and dangerously, into the sea right ahead of the ship. Sometimes erratic rockets exploded and injured the crew.

None of these calamities happened to Varley. At 1510, only three minutes after identification of the Focke-Wulf, he was airborne from a perfect launch directly into the wind, all thirteen rockets in the cluster having fired.

The Condor had evidently seen him or the flash of the rockets, for it dived to sea level to hide among the wave tops in its grey-green chameleon's camouflage, and neither Varley nor Gostelow in the *Empire Foam* could see it at first. Then it was sighted between five and ten miles astern of the convoy. Varley thought that the FW was playing decoy, and decided to patrol astern of the convoy.

There were two other CAM-ships in the convoy, both fitted with RDF, which *Empire Foam* did not have. Gostelow called them up but neither of them had a plot of the snooper. While he was doing this a destroyer relayed a message from the Senior Officer Escort that there was an enemy five miles astern of the convoy. Varley flew to investigate, but found nothing.

After he had been on patrol for another forty minutes Gostelow called him up to report another possibly hostile aircraft in his vicinity. Varley saw one of the corvettes of the escort firing her light ack-ack guns and looking in the direction of the puffs of smoke saw a large four-engined aircraft dead ahead of the convoy. Then he recognised it as a Liberator, which fired the colours of the day when it sighted the Hurricane.

Varley returned to the convoy, patrolled uneventfully for a while, then called up the *Empire Foam* and informed Gostelow that his petrol gauges told him that he must bale out in about twenty minutes. As the time ran out he picked out the nearest escort vessel, the destroyer *Broke*, and circled her, rocking the Hurricane to signal his intention of baling out. Then he climbed to 3,000 feet and prepared to abandon the aircraft. It took him some time to jettison the emergency release panel. At last he managed to push it out. He pushed his flaps down, throttled back, got his feet out on the starboard wing, and jumped. It was 1708, and he had been in the air for very nearly two hours. The Hurricane, with twenty gallons of fuel left in the tanks and full ammunition belts in the guns, crashed in the sea and was lost.

On his own way down Varley inflated his Mae West. He hit the water, the parachute filled with wind and dragged him for a few yards on his stomach. Luckily the sea was still calm. He opened the CO_2 bottle on his Mae West, inflated his dinghy and struggled into it. Almost immediately the grey bulk of the *Broke* came alongside him. A man threw him a line and he was hauled aboard. After a hot bath and a cup of tea well laced with rum, Varley felt reasonably normal, though chagrined at the escape of the Focke-Wulf. But if the FW had escaped, so had the convoy. Before Varley chased it away the Condor had been seen to open its bomb doors in preparation for a run in on a straggler astern and to port of the convoy.

Focke-Wulf Condor 200C-4

5

The loss of a good Hurricane after Varley's sortie was to be deplored, and Hawkers gave a lot of thought to means of saving the CAM aircraft—as well as giving the pilot a better chance of survival—after an operation. When a Hurricane was ditched it was not really worth picking up. Even if it could be made to float long enough, once salt water got into the fuselage and wings only an immediate major overhaul could make it operational again, and this would not be possible. The fitting of floats was considered but discarded as they would seriously spoil the machine's performance. Another idea was the removal of the undercarriage and the fitting of an extra petrol tank in the undercarriage bay, but this meant that should the aircraft be within reach of land it could only crash-land, with probable serious damage. But in the autumn of 1941 the CAM-ship Hurricanes were fitted with 44-gallon drop tanks. The extra range prolonged the pilot's combat time and gave him a better chance of reaching land or a friendly ship after a combat, though the added weight did reduce his manoeuvrability in combat and necessitated a boosting of the catapult's launching power. The two-seat Fulmar, although having the advantage of being able to carry an observer/navigator, had proved too slow for combat, and all the catapult ships had standardised on the Sea Hurricane.

On October 29th the *Empire Audacity* had begun another run to Gibraltar with OG76, a convoy of twenty ships. Winter gales were raging in the Atlantic and the weather gave the eight Martlets which *Audacity* now carried some very rough handling. Sometimes the carrier's flight deck pitched sixty-five feet, as measured by sextant, with the ship rolling sixteen degrees. Sub-Lieutenant Patterson's Martlet was struck, as he was touching down, by the after end of the flight deck on an upswing. The aircraft missed the wires and skidded over the port side. The Martlet was lost but flotation bags in its wings inflated and kept the machine afloat long enough for Patterson to be rescued by an escort vessel.

Sea Hurricane leaving the catapult

On the day after this *Audacity*'s radar picked up an unidentified aircraft near the convoy. 802 Squadron's Commanding Officer, Lieutenant Commander Wintour, RN, and Sub-Lieutenant D. A. Hutchison, RN, investigated and found a Condor shadowing the convoy. Wintour made two quarter attacks and seeing the FW badly on fire, thought that the combat was over. As he flew in closer to make sure, the FW's upper gunner opened up on him with cannon fire. A shell hit Wintour's cockpit and he was killed. Hutchison, a Battle of Britain pilot, took over the attack and shot down the Condor.

By this time the little squadron had suffered badly from attrition by the weather, accidents and enemy action, and when another unidentified aircraft was picked up that afternoon there was only one really serviceable aircraft left, although there was another with a bent airscrew caused by some clumsy plane handling by the flight deck party. Lamb and Brown were the readiness section, and Brown volunteered to fly the damaged machine.

The target turned out to be the American Dixie Clipper flying boat, but as they were flying back to the convoy Lamb sighted two Condors. He attacked one and Brown the other.

Both FW's used the thick cloud to try to shake off the Martlets. Brown got in three short bursts and set the starboard inner engine of his Condor on fire, then the big machine disappeared in the cloud. Brown held on through the cloud. It began to thin out and suddenly he saw the Condor coming at him head on. He opened fire and saw his bullets shatter the cockpit windscreen, then had to pull up violently to avoid collision. The FW crashed into the sea. Brown returned to *Audacity* with his engine running very rough.

On December 14th *Audacity* sailed from Gibraltar as part of Commander F. J. Walker's 36th Escort Group, which had a powerful force of sixteen escort vessels in addition to the carrier to look after thirty-two merchantmen. *Audacity* carried just four serviceable Martlets. On the 17th, when the convoy was out of

Trial launch of a Sea Hurricane in harbour

CAM-ship pilots with their Fighter Direction Officer aboard Empire Tide.
Left: *Flying Officer Fenwick;* right: *Flight Lieutenant Turley-George*

range of air cover by Swordfish from Gibraltar, Sub-Lieutenant Fletcher was ordered by Commander Walker to attack a surfaced U-boat which had been sighted by another Martlet and prevent her from diving long enough for the surface escorts to come up. The U-boat made no attempt to dive as the Martlet approached but fought it out with her guns. Just as Fletcher opened fire with his Brownings a shell hit his windscreen and he was killed. Then three of Walker's sloops opened fire and in twenty minutes the U-boat had been destroyed.

Two of the surviving three Martlets flown by Hutchison and the new CO, Lieutenant Gibson, attacked a Focke-Wulf on the 18th but the guns of both machines jammed as they came in to attack. A hard battle now developed between Walker's escorts and the U-boats and Focke-Wulfs.

The U-boats were in wolf pack strength. The sloop *Stanley* was torpedoed on the 18th and blew up. Captain Walker's ship *Stork* attacked with depth charges and forced *U-574* to the surface, then rammed and sank her. The leading merchantman in the port column of the convoy was torpedoed and sunk. An hour later *Audacity* was narrowly missed by a torpedo.

On the morning of the 19th when all the carrier's remaining three Martlets were in the air they intercepted three FW 200's. Brown shot down one in a head on attack, and Lamb damaged another. In the afternoon *Stork* sighted another FW snooper and alerted *Audacity*. Lieutenant J. W. Sleigh, RN, and Sub-

Lieutenant H. E. Williams, RNVR, scrambled and attacked it. They made several stern attacks with no effect so Sleigh tried a head on attack. The Condor went down out of control. Sleigh was so close when he pulled up to avoid collision that he hit the FW's port wing tip. He returned to *Audacity* with its aileron dangling from his tail wheel.

At 2037 on the 20th, an hour after the dusk patrol had made a very difficult landing in the dark, a torpedo hit *Audacity* right aft on the port side. She went down by the stern until the 4-inch gun platform was awash. The rudder was damaged and the ship was not under command, so Commander McKendrick stopped engines to avoid colliding with other ships, and waited for a tow.

Twenty minutes later their attacker, *U-751*, surfaced two hundred yards from *Audacity* on her port beam. A lone gunner on the carrier opened fire on the U-boat with his Oerlikon. Then two white tracks were spotted coming straight for the stricken ship. The torpedoes blew *Audacity*'s bows off, and her stern reared into the air, her aircraft bursting their lashings and careering down the tilting flight deck, wrecking those lifeboats and rafts which had not already been destroyed. Men jumped from her promenade deck and flight deck catwalk into the sea. *Audacity* tilted further, her single screw high in the air, then plunged to the bottom, internal explosions rumbling under-water.

Survivors were picked up by corvettes of the escort, but losses were heavy, including Commander McKendrick and two of the pilots.

While she lasted *Empire Audacity* had been effective. Her fighters had shot down five Condors and damaged three. These were losses which *II Gruppe* could not afford. Her Martlets had also been of some assistance in sighting U-boats, and had contributed to the four which Walker's escorts had sunk.

But now, after only two round-trips, she was gone. Two of the Fighter Catapult Ships had also been knocked out in other convoy battles. Other, better, escort carriers were being built, but the first of these would not be finished until the following spring at the very earliest. Until then the Hurricats of the CAM-ships, and the two remaining Fighter Catapult Ships would be the convoys' only fighter protection in mid-ocean. And U-boat strength would be increasing rapidly all the time.

6

As it happened the North Atlantic and Gibraltar convoys were spared the full fury of the U-boats during the early months of 1942. On December 7th, 1941, four days after Pearl Harbour, Germany declared war on the United States, and switched most of her U-boats to attacks on the great, virtually unprotected stream of shipping passing up and down the east coast of America, carrying petrol and oil from the Gulf of Mexico for American industry and for the Allied war effort, aluminium ore from Brazil and the Guianas. This vital pipeline was severely damaged. In the January of 1942 the U-boats sank 320,000 tons of Allied shipping, in February about 500,000 tons. Most of this was off the American coast or in the Caribbean.

The Gibraltar convoys, temporarily spared heavy U-boat attack, were now suffering increasingly severe attacks by land-based aircraft. In February, 1942, the FW 200C-3 was superseded by the C-4. The C-4 was the best version of the Condor and the one produced in the largest numbers. Carrying its standard fuel load of 1,773 Imperial gallons, and flying at its economical cruising speed of 158 mph, it had a range of 2,210 miles. With 2,190 gallons this was stretched to 2,760 miles. It had a top speed at 15,750 feet of 224 mph and 190 mph at sea level, with a top cruising speed of 208 mph at 13,120 feet and 172 mph at sea level. Bomb load was the same as the C-3's, but it carried one more gun, a 13-millimetre machine-gun with 500 rounds in a flexible mounting, in an upper position aft, in addition to the C-3's forward dorsal 7.9 millimetre machine-gun with 1,000 rounds, two 13-millimetres with 300 rounds at the beam hatches, and in the belly gondola the 7.9 with 1,000 rounds and the 20-millimetre cannon with 500 rounds.

Early C-4's were fitted with FuG *Rostock* search radar, which was largely superseded by the FuG *Hohentwiel* type. *Rostock*, with a wider search angle and a greater range, was adequate for a general shipping search, to be followed up by

CAM-ship and Sea Hurricane after safe arrival in a North African port

low-level attack, but could not pinpoint targets with any accuracy at ranges below three miles. *Hohentwiel* worked on a smaller scale and could isolate targets at under a mile, which made it the better type to use in the high-level, 'blind-bombing' tactics which became progressively more popular as pickings became harder.

The Condors worked two main patrol areas. A 'limited recce' went as far north as 45°, an 'extended recce' out to 34°, with a normal westerly limit in both cases of 19° West, sometimes 25°. Condors on a routine search flew low and kept in formation for mutual protection until they reached the search area, then they split up and worked singly. A typical search pattern was the *Fächer*, or Fan, in which an aircraft covered a corridor of ocean in a zig-zag, turning 90° each time it altered course, to port and starboard alternately.

The rate of production of the new escort carriers was much slower than expected, and even those which would be ready in 1942 were already reserved for a major assault on the coast of North Africa planned for later that year and for other similar operations in 1943. Alternatives had to be found.

The Admiralty turned to Captain Slattery's idea for a merchant ship aircraft carrier which could continue to carry its normal cargo, a big brother in fact of the CAM-ship. A scheme was discussed to adapt two grain ships, which were loaded through trunk hoses and had no deck loading arrangements which would prevent the fitting of a flight deck. It was thought that each of these $10\frac{1}{2}$–12 knot ships of 7,000–8,000 tons could operate three or four torpedo-spotter-reconnaissance aircraft, although various types of machine were investigated, including the American Vought-Sikorsky OS2-U Kingfisher, a two-seat reconnaissance monoplane in either landplane or floatplane form, which could carry 240 pounds of bombs and cruise at 150 mph, with a range of 900 miles.

In March 1942 at a meeting of the Tanker Tonnage Committee of the Petroleum Board in Shell-Mex House, the Chairman told the members that the Admiralty were thinking of these grain ship conversions. Immediately, John Lamb, Marine Superintendent of the Anglo-Saxon Petroleum Company and an ex-ship's engineer already distinguished as an inventor and improviser of maritime equipment in wartime, said, 'But what about doing it with tankers?' Oil, like grain, was piped into a ship, and offered no obstacles to the fitting of a flight deck.

The Committee were enthusiastic, and Lamb and his staff began working out practical details. Lamb himself had become particularly depressed by the terrible losses among tankers, many of them containing old shipmates, and the idea of actually providing them with their own protective aircraft became a crusade for him.

By this time the Russian convoy situation had begun to change. The Germans had realised that the war against Russia was going to be much longer and harder than they had anticipated. The importance of the supply route from Britain to Russia thus became greatly increased. The main surface units of the German Navy were sent to Norwegian waters. A flotilla of U-boats and large numbers of dive-bombers and torpedo aircraft were sent to northern Norway to destroy the convoys to Russia. The hours of daylight were now increasing, and ice would force the convoys to pass close to the enemy occupied coast for two or three more months. Among the Luftwaffe units moved to Norway was the original Condor squadron to operate from Bordeaux-Merignac, which was transferred to Trondheim-Vaernes, leaving one squadron to continue operations from Bordeaux.

On March 1st, 1942, outward bound convoy PQ12 sailed from Iceland and homeward bound QP8 from Kola Inlet. On the 5th a Focke-Wulf reported the position of PQ12. The battleship *Tirpitz* and three destroyers sailed from Trondheim to attack it. They missed the convoy, but the Home Fleet missed them. Albacore torpedo bombers from the Fleet carrier *Victorious* attacked but failed to hit the *Tirpitz*. On March 20th PQ13 left Reykjavik and on the 21st QP9 sailed from Murmansk, each with nineteen ships. QP9 had a safe voyage, but PQ13 was hit by gales and by greatly increased enemy action. Two stragglers were sunk by bombs, two by U-boats, and one by a destroyer. The cruiser *Trinidad* and the destroyer *Eclipse* were badly damaged. In PQ15, which sailed at the end of April, torpedo bombers sank three merchant ships, and a Junkers 88 sank the repaired *Trinidad*. The cruiser *Edinburgh* and three British destroyers were also lost during the battle. There was a CAM-ship, the *Empire Morn*, with this convoy, but her Hurricane was not in action.

The need for fighters with the convoy escorts was urgent. When PQ16, with thirty-five ships the largest Russian convoy so far, sailed from Iceland on May 15th it included a CAM-ship, the *Empire Lawrence*. Sailing simultaneously from Murmansk, QP12 included the *Empire Morn*. It was the best that could be done.

At about 0300 in the morning of the 25th, when the two convoys were drawing close to one another, a Focke-Wulf 200 was spotted about ten miles off circling PQ16, then north-west of Trondheim. The aircraft continued to watch the convoy. The weather was too cloudy and misty for the *Empire Lawrence*'s Hurricane to be launched.

Empire Audacity

Aboard the *Empire Morn* in QP12, Pilot Officer Faulks had the 2400–0600 watch. About 0545 a flying boat, identified as a Blohm und Voss Br 138, appeared on the horizon and proceeded to circle the convoy at a distance of about twelve miles. About 0700 a FW 200 appeared. The Blohm und Voss made a recognition signal of two red flashes, and the Focke-Wulf joined in the patrol of the convoy. The weather round QP12 was improving, and approval to launch the aircraft was asked for from the command ship, HMS *Ulster Queen*, which was on RDF watch, by *Empire Morn*'s Master, Captain W. L. Cruickshank, but a delay was suggested until further enemy aircraft were sighted.

At 0600 Flying Officer J. B. Kendal relieved Pilot Officer Faulks and was strapped into the Hurricane's cockpit. Faulks connected the safety link and satisfied himself that the catapult was clear. He had the clamps and safety bar removed from the trolley, leaving only the pins in position.

About 0830 a Junkers 88 appeared, then another. There were now four enemy aircraft circling QP12 independently. Faulks and the Master agreed that it was time to launch. Kendal concurred but asked them to wait for a moment when the enemy were ahead or astern, so that there would be less chance of their seeing the flash of the rockets. Surprise could help to reduce the odds of four well armed enemy machines to one Hurricane.

At approximately 0850 one Junkers 88 was ahead of the convoy and hidden in a patch of rain cloud, the other three enemy aircraft were astern. The ship hoisted the Aeroplane Flag. Faulks signalled Kendal to start up, and removed the safety pins. Faulks held up his blue flag. Captain Cruickshank answered with his blue flag. Faulks took a last look round to assure himself that everything was in order, and started to rotate his blue flag in the air. Kendal opened up and locked the throttle, raised his hand. Faulks counted to three, and moved the switch.

Nothing happened. Faulks waved his red flag, which was seen by Kendal and the Master, then examined the safety link and found the connection at one end slightly loose. He tightened it and made sure the points were making full contact. He repeated his drill with the blue flag, received the 'ready' signal from the pilot, counted to three and moved the switch.

Twelve of the thirteen rockets fired and the Hurricane made a good launch into a very light wind, hardly sinking at all when it went off the bows. The pilot turned to port and began to climb steadily, and the Fighter Direction Officer, Sub-Lieutenant P. G. Mallett, vectored him to engage the Blohm und Voss at nine o'clock. The flying boat did not seem to have seen the launch, as it had maintained its steady course. Raising his flaps, Kendal vanished into the rain cloud. Just then the thirteenth rocket in the cluster, which had failed on launching, blew with a bang and a flash, set off by conducted heat from the other rockets.

For some five minutes Kendal was lost to view, and Faulks kept watch on the

Grumman Martlets of the Fleet Air Arm

trolley while the rockets burned out. A fire hose which had been connected up and held in reserve in case of fire was used to cool down the rocket tubes. Faulks satisfied himself that there was no danger of fire, then left the trolley and the catapult in the hands of the crew and joined the FDO on the bridge. Mallett said that he was having difficulty communicating with Kendal. He had transmitted 'Return to control' on R/T but there had been no acknowledgement and the pilot had not answered any of his signals. They learned later that he had received them all and acknowledged them, but that they could not receive him over ranges greater than half a mile. Mallett had the RDF activated to get a fix on the Hurricane.

Then it was spotted on the port quarter rapidly closing a Ju 88, which was still circling the convoy in an anti-clockwise direction at a height of about 1,000 feet, speed about 200 mph. When the 88 was astern of the convoy they saw the Hurricane attack, first from starboard, then port, opening fire at two hundred yards. They heard two long bursts of fire.

It was a perfectly timed attack and must have taken the enemy completely by surprise, as there was no answering fire from the enemy rear gunner. The Junkers appeared to stagger in the air, then black smoke poured from one engine. The German pilot tried desperately to maintain height by keeping the nose up. The machine limped along the starboard side of the convoy, one engine completely dead, the other misfiring badly. Through their binoculars Faulks, Mallett and Cruickshank watched the crew jettisoning everything they could, including the bombs. The machine continued to lose height and speed. It disappeared from the view of the watchers on the bridge of the *Empire Morn*. Then they saw smoke on the horizon at Green 45°.

Then the Hurricane came out of the clouds on the starboard bow. As he approached the convoy Kendal fired a recognition signal to one of the destroyers of the escort. Mallett tried the R/T again and this time the pilot's voice came through. He reported that he had used up all his ammunition but could give no final result of his attack. Mallett suggested that he fly over to see what had become of the Junkers. Kendal flew off towards the smoke.

Presently he returned and told them that he had seen wreckage floating on the surface about eight miles from the convoy, with a rubber dinghy close by. He could not see whether there had been anyone in the dinghy or not. Mallett congratulated him on behalf of everyone for his fine performance. Kendal thanked him then flew off towards one of the leading destroyer escorts, the *Boadicea*.

Kendal had had a previous arrangement to be picked up by this ship, but the convoy was now heading into a patch of bad visibility. Mallett warned Kendal about this and suggested that he choose one of the rear escort vessels and bale out. Although Kendal did not acknowledge this signal, they saw him fly over the ships and begin orbiting the *Badsworth*, a destroyer on the starboard quarter of the convoy. The *Empire Morn*'s Aldis lamp was out of action, so all the escort ships were told by R/T 'Stand by to pick up pilot'.

Kendal continued to orbit the *Badsworth* for a few minutes on a left-hand circuit, rocking his aircraft. Faulks then saw him fly astern of the destroyer, turn round, and fly back over and on the same course as the destroyer, climbing into the cloud base, which was at about seven hundred feet.

They heard Kendal climbing for about thirty seconds. By this time he was well ahead of the ship and at a height of between 1,000 and 1,200 feet. Faulks heard the Hurricane's airscrew go into fully fine pitch, followed by the sudden cutting of the engine, then silence. A few seconds later the aircraft dropped out of the cloud, with the figure of Kendal falling close alongside it, his parachute only half open. The Hurricane plunged into the sea in a vertical dive. Only fifty feet from the sea Kendal's parachute opened. The aircraft sank immediately, and all they could see of Kendal was the yellow canopy of his parachute floating on the water. The *Badsworth* raced to the spot, lowering a boat as she came up. The boat was seen to heave to by the parachute, then return to the destroyer to be hoisted inboard. A few minutes later, about 1010, the *Badsworth* called up the *Empire Morn* by Aldis lamp and told them that Kendal had been picked up with very serious injuries. Some ten minutes after this came the news that he had died and would be buried at sea at 1400.

Faulks thought that Kendal must have tried to abandon the Hurricane by the 'Jack in the Box' method, which entailed the sudden cutting of the engine and a vertical dive. He had perhaps been injured getting clear, or in some way been unable to pull the ripcord until it was too late for the parachute to break the shock of the impact with the sea. He had not complained of being wounded in the action with the Junkers 88.

It was a very sad end to a brilliant display of flying skill and courage. But the result, in addition to the destruction of the Ju 88, was that the remaining enemy machines scattered and none were sighted again, although the convoy was within range of them for the next twenty-four hours.

That afternoon QP12 passed PQ16, and shortly afterwards a full scale air attack developed against the latter. Heinkel III torpedo bombers alternated with Ju 88 dive-bombers. Murky weather had dogged PQ16, and it was too misty and cloudy to launch the Hurricane against the persistent FW200 which had remained in attendance. Then about 1600 in the afternoon the sky cleared.

At 1845 Pilot Officer Hay was in the *Empire Lawrence*'s Sea Hurricane. The RDF had not been switched on, and when six Ju 88's flew right over the convoy at about 6,000 feet, going east to west in two formations of three, it was too late for the Hurricane to catch them up, so it was not launched. They began to drop bombs indiscriminately. The RDF was then belatedly switched on and at once picked up a number of enemy aircraft approaching from dead ahead about fifteen miles distant. Minutes later lookouts on deck saw five enemy aircraft in line astern at wide intervals, flying at about a hundred feet from the sea towards the convoy from the west, with the leader about ten miles away. The guns of the escorts opened fire.

Hay gave the readiness signal. The *Empire Lawrence* turned into wind, and the Hurricane made a good take-off. Hay at once closed in on the German machines, recognising them as Heinkel III's. They saw the Hurricane, closed in to vic formation and turned sharply away northward.

Hawker Sea Hurricanes on the flight deck in bad weather

The Escort Carrier HMS Avenger

The last Heinkel on the starboard side of the formation was straggling slightly. Hay came in on its quarter firing two bursts of about three seconds each from slightly above the enemy at about two hundred and fifty yards, closing in. He saw red flashes near the Heinkel's starboard engine and pieces fall off it. The Heinkel had closed up in formation by now and the Hurricane came under fire from the dorsal guns of all five enemy machines, none of which hit him.

Hay then broke away to starboard and climbed for another attack. He made a quarter attack on the enemy Number Two aircraft, firing one five-second burst from two hundred and fifty yards. He came under a storm of return fire but was able to see his own bullets hitting the Heinkel abaft the cockpit before the Hurricane was hit in the glycol tank. Temporarily blinded by the glycol he broke away. As he was doing so 'a small explosive missile', as Hay called it, penetrated the cockpit, exploding against the seat with a white puff, and a piece of metal hit him in the leg. A plane flashed momentarily into his sights and he spent the rest of his 2,640 mixed De Wilde and armour-piercing rounds on it. He thought it was a Ju 88.

Then he broke away and decided to bale out, as his engine was overheating badly through lack of coolant. He flew towards the convoy and told the FDO in *Empire Lawrence* that he intended to bale out. He climbed to about 3,000 feet over the starboard side of the convoy but at once noticed a section of Ju 88's coming in from the west. He crossed to the port side of the convoy, where there was less enemy action, jettisoned his hood, throttled back, lowered his flaps, and baled out.

He splashed down and tried to inflate his dinghy, but discovered it was punctured. It sank almost at once, but within six minutes of hitting the water

FAIREY SWORDFISH

Width: 62 Ft.

Hangar Hoist.

Flight Deck: 422 Ft.

Personnal.

Wheel House on starboard side.

Hangar.

8 Cargo Holds.

Diesel Engine Room.

Water ballast, oil Fuel and fresh water.

A grain ship converted into a Merchant Aircraft Carrier—from The Illustrated London News

he was picked up by the destroyer *Volunteer*, although the destroyer was under violent attack by the enemy. The Gunnery Officer of the *Volunteer* confirmed that Hay's first Heinkel had crashed into the sea. The shell which had penetrated his cockpit had come from one of the convoy's own ships. Some gunners on American freighters, inexperienced in aircraft recognition, were firing at anything that flew. The Hurricane may have been hit by some of these trigger-happy shots. *Carlton* fired at it. Men in the merchant ships saw the Hurricane fall blazing into the sea.

The Luftwaffe claimed to have destroyed PQ16, and Admiral Doenitz himself recommended that aircraft, without U-boats, should be used against the summer convoys. In fact five merchantmen were sunk, including the *Empire Lawrence*. Six bombers concentrated on her. When they had finished there was nothing left of the CAM-ship but one damaged lifeboat and a few survivors in a pool of oil. One other merchantman and the destroyer *Garland* were badly damaged. The convoy arrived at Kola Inlet with 125,000 tons of supplies, having lost 147 tanks out of 468, 77 aircraft out of 201, 770 other vehicles out of 3,277. It could have been very much worse.

Commander R. Onslow, Senior Officer Escort of PQ16, urged that many more CAM-ships or an escort carrier and more anti-aircraft ships be included in the next convoys. Arrangements were started for Coastal Command to operate from Russian bases. The enemy had on airfields round the North Cape of Norway 103 Ju 88's, 42 Heinkel III's, 15 He.115's, 30 Stukas and 74 long-range aircraft comprising FW 200's, Ju 88's and Blohm und Voss Br 138's. These would be ready for the next convoy.

7

The Luftwaffe were continuing to harry the Gibraltar convoys as well. On June 14th, 1942, a Focke-Wulf 200 attacked a homeward bound convoy. Pilot Officer Saunders was launched from the CAM-ship *Empire Moon*, leading the port column of ships, and shot it down. Saunders then ditched his Hurricane. The Hurricane hit the water on its back. Saunders struggled out and clung to the wing for about three-quarters of a minute until the machine sank. Then he was on his own in a leaking dinghy. Four minutes later however he was picked up.

Thirty-one escort carriers were now on order, but the first of these would not be ready before the autumn and the rest only in ones and twos over the following months, with urgent commitments elsewhere when they were ready. In this situation the Admiralty gave the go-ahead for the conversion of two grain-carrying ships to operate aircraft as well as continue to carry cargo. The Burntisland Shipping Company was asked to draw up the detailed plans and carry out the work. The Admiralty wanted a minimum flight deck length of 490 feet and a speed of 14–15 knots, but had to lower their standards to 10½–12 knots and 390 feet so that war standard cargo hulls could be used.

The Fairey Swordfish, and not after all the Vought-Sikorsky Kingfisher, was finally selected for use aboard these ships. Although, with a cruising speed of 90–100 knots it was 50 mph slower than the Kingfisher, and its range with a bomb load was smaller, it had advantages over the more sophisticated American machine which made it suitable for the slow vessels, with their abbreviated flight decks and small hangar space and nothing but the most basic facilities for repair and maintenance.

The design of the Swordfish went back to 1932, when an attempt had been made to clarify and streamline the then muddled functions performed by the heterogeneous collection of British naval aircraft. On the suggestion of a carrier captain in the Mediterranean a specification was drafted for a torpedo-bomber-spotter-reconnaissance aircraft, which would combine all the functions except that of the fighter in one type. The machine which this produced was a maid-of-all-work versatile beyond any aviator's dreams.

The prototype No. F.1875 of the Fairey Swordfish, a two-seater, first flew on March 21st, 1933. On September 11th it crashed in a flat spin. The design was later changed to incorporate an extra bay and a third seat in the fuselage towards the tail, and the Swordfish ousted its rival the Blackburn Shark as first-line strike aircraft for the Naval Air Arm.

By 1939 the stately biplane with a top speed of 139 mph had been completely outclassed and made to look ridiculous by the sleek monoplane bombers of the United States and Japanese Navies. But owing to the gross neglect of naval aviation by the British Government it was still the best in British service. And in practice it served well. Swordfish had stopped the *Bismarck*, crippled the Italian Fleet at Taranto, searched millions of miles of ocean for raiders, fought Me 109's over Dunkirk and in Norwegian fiords.

The old 'Stringbags', were slow, but they were tolerant of ham-fisted young pilots. Their stability and slow landing speed of about 60 knots made them ideal deck-landers for the small carriers, which could be very lively in rough weather. They could be pulled off the deck and put straight into a climbing turn at 55 knots. Their speed in a dive never rose much above 200 knots, which left the crew exposed too long to anti-aircraft fire for comfort but otherwise made for accuracy of bombing, and they could hold the dive as low as 200 feet. Their normal range was 546 miles, but this could be extended with extra fuel and a lighter bomb load. They could still be effective against submarines, with bombs or depth-charges, and when rockets were first successfully fired from a Swordfish at Thorney Island on October 12th, 1942, they took on a new lease of life as U-boat hunters. They were cheap to build, and expendable.

Four Stringbags would be carried in each grainer-carrier. These ships would fly the Red Ensign and be known as Merchant Aircraft Carriers. It was hoped that they would stop the gap, as it ought to be possible to complete them in less than half the time needed to build an escort carrier.

The Admiralty were less impressed with John Lamb's scheme for the similar conversion of tankers into Merchant Aircraft Carriers. Lamb had decided, after consulting an expert on carrier operations, that Anglo-Saxon Petroleum's 12,000 tons deadweight tankers were suitable for rapid conversion. His plans were passed by the Tanker Tonnage Committee and sent to the Admiralty. Lamb was sent for to discuss them with Admiralty and Ministry of War Transport officials, who raised objections on the grounds of fire risk. They thought that an

aircraft might crash into the ship's superstructure, or even through the flight deck, and set the ship on fire. A valuable ship, cargo and crew might be lost, they argued, and the resulting column of smoke and flame attract Focke-Wulfs and U-boats into the bargain. They were concerned too about the attendant psychological effects of such a risk upon the ship's company.

Lamb thought these objections unrealistic. His naval flying expert told him that aircraft were unlikely to crash in this way, and he felt sure from his own experience that fire was far less of a risk than the officials imagined. As for psychological effects, seamen would trust their officers not to accept foolhardy risks. He proposed flooding the flight decks during flying operations, and said that he was 'quite happy to convert even a benzine ship.' Discussions of his

In May 1943 Lieutenant Commander R. W. Slater flew a Swordfish aboard the Merchant Aircraft Carrier Empire MacAlpine, *the first time an aircraft had ever landed on a merchant ship. In the near picture he is seen shaking hands with Mr. Campbell, First Officer of the* Empire MacAlpine

scheme continued, and an idea was also explored for converting the *Queen Mary* and *Queen Elizabeth*, then on troop-carrying duty, and possibly the *Mauretania*, into aircraft carriers.

None of these emergency schemes would bear fruit in time to help the summer Russian convoys. When PQ17 sailed for Russia in late June it had as close escorts six destroyers, two anti-aircraft ships and two submarines, with corvettes, trawlers and rescue ships, but only one CAM-ship, the *Empire Tide*, to provide air cover. At a brief meeting just before the convoy sailed Rear Admiral Hamilton, commanding a covering force of cruisers which would accompany the convoy part of the way, discussed the role of the CAM-ship with its senior pilot, Turley-George, and it was decided that the Hurricane could be most usefully employed against a serious bombing attack, rather than be launched against a shadower, the loss of which would be negligible to the Germans. Hamilton ordered a wooden dummy Hurricane to be built, which could be sat on the catapult when the genuine article had been launched, as a deterrent. The Home Fleet was also to cover the convoy as far as a point between Bear Island and North Cape. After that PQ17 would be on its own, with the *Tirpitz, Scheer, Luetzow, Hipper* and twelve destroyers poised to attack it. Luftwaffe strength had also been further increased. Daylight would be almost continuous and the polar ice pack had not yet receded, so the convoy would have to pass within easy striking distance of the enemy's bombers.

On July 4th, when PQ17 was between Bear Island and North Cape, the First Lord of the Admiralty, Sir Dudley Pound, fearing that the German heavy ships were about to pounce on the convoy, ordered it to scatter and proceed independently to Archangel. The attack by German surface ships was called off, but the almost defenceless merchantmen were decimated by bombers and submarines. Of the thirty-five merchant ships, fourteen were sunk by air attack, ten by U-boats. One of the survivors was the *Empire Tide*, which arrived in Archangel on July 24th with its aircraft still on the catapult. The Hurricane had gone to action stations when a Junkers 88 had flown round the ship at a great height while she was hiding in a rocky harbour on the coast of Novaya Zemlya, and the engine had been run up, but the Junkers made off.

Losses on this scale were unacceptable. If the convoys were to continue they had to have air cover. The North Atlantic and Gibraltar routes were also facing this urgent need once again. Allied shipping sunk by U-boats reached a total of 700,000 tons in June 1942, most of these in American coastal waters, but in July the Americans had almost completed their convoy system. Sinkings by U-boat in these waters declined dramatically, and the U-boats there were switched back to the Atlantic convoy routes. Soon there were between seventy and eighty of them there, most of them concentrated against the North Atlantic convoys. German aircraft continued to inflict heavy losses on Gibraltar convoys as well. The need for air escorts was growing more and more urgent. If the U-boats in the Atlantic should achieve anything like their rate of sinkings off the American coasts, Britain was in danger of losing the Battle of the Atlantic.

The stop-gaps, the catapult ships, did what they could. About fifteen North Atlantic convoys, usually of between thirty and sixty merchantmen each, were entering port each month, and about 2,500,000 tons of shipping were being turned round at British ports monthly. One CAM-ship, sometimes two, was included in as many of these convoys as possible and in those going to Gibraltar and Malta, which was also under heavy attack by the Luftwaffe.

Improvements had been made in anti-U-boat techniques since the Atlantic battles of 1941. The new direction-finding sets could take the bearings of the high-frequency intercommunication in a wolf pack. Ahead-throwing weapons gave better results than dropped depth-charges. Long range aircraft patrols from Britain, America and Canada had been increased. But there was still no more than token aircraft coverage in the 500-mile mid-Atlantic Gap.

For the next convoy to Russia, PQ18, the Admiralty waited until September, when at least there would be several hours of darkness each night and long periods of twilight, and the polar ice would have receded to its northernmost position, so that the convoy would be able to pass north of Bear Island and about three hundred miles off Norway.

For protection against all forms of attack this convoy of thirty-nine merchant-men had a very much stronger close escort. Besides the normal close escort of

The grain ship/Merchant Aircraft Carrier Empire MacRae *in convoy*

sloops, corvettes and mine-sweepers, there was a special 'fighting destroyer escort' of sixteen Fleet destroyers and, at last, an escort carrier, the *Avenger*, with twelve Sea Hurricanes and three Swordfish. The escort force was commanded by Rear-Admiral R. L. Burnett, with his flag in the cruiser *Scylla*, which was fitted out as an anti-aircraft cruiser.

Thirteen Catalina flying boats and twenty-three torpedo-carrying Hampdens were sent to North Russia to give cover to PQ18 on the last stage, and at the same time cover a homeward bound convoy. Included among the merchant ships was the veteran CAM-ship *Empire Morn*, from which Flying Officer Kendal had flown his successful, and tragic, sortie. Commodore of the convoy was Rear-Admiral E. K. Boddam-Whetham, DSO, who had been the first officer of the rank of Commander to qualify as an observer in the Fleet Air Arm after World War I.

When the convoy sailed from Loch Ewe on September 2nd it was known that the German Fifth Air Fleet in Norway had been strengthened in preparation for further Arctic convoys by the transfer of Heinkel III's, which carried two torpedoes apiece, Ju 88 dive-bombers and Focke-Wulf Condors. This gave the Luftwaffe approximately 300 operational bombers, including 92 torpedo bombers and 133 long-range and dive-bombers, to use against PQ18, with Me 109's as fighter escort.

As protection for a convoy against this sort of large-scale attack a single small carrier like the *Avenger*, with only twelve Sea Hurricanes and three Swordfish, was an unknown quantity. Although *Audacity*'s Martlets had done great work in the defence of their convoys, two or three Condors were the most they had had to deal with in the air. As to whether carriers could break the tyranny of shore-based aircraft over ships, the inevitable forthcoming duel hardly looked as if it would be a fair test. But twelve Sea Hurricanes should be better than one, which was literally all that most of the best protected convoys had had hitherto.

Six of these aircraft comprised 802 Squadron, the old *Empire Audacity* unit, which had re-formed with five of the *Audacity* survivors at Yeovilton on February 1st, 1942. When they embarked in *Avenger* they joined the six Sea Hurricanes of No. 883 Squadron, which had been re-formed in the previous October. Their machines had had both catapult spools and deck arrester hooks fitted; their air frames had been strengthened by General Aircraft at Feltham in Middlesex, and they were now re-designated Sea Hurricane IB's.

In planning their tactics it was decided that, contrary to the conclusion arrived at in the discussion between Rear-Admiral Hamilton and the pilot of the

Empire Tide's Hurricane before the sailing of PQ17, the Hurricanes should go all out to destroy German shadowing aircraft when they first appeared, with the idea of concealing the convoy's movements from the enemy.

Patrolling U-boats were the first to give warning of a convoy's approach. On their information German heavy warships sailed from Bergen on September 6th, when PQ18 was passing Jan Mayen Island. Once again they failed to connect with their target and turned back. On the 9th the *Scylla*, *Avenger* and half the destroyer force joined the convoy. The convoy was picked up by a shadowing aircraft. On the 10th U-boats began their attacks. On the 12th, when PQ18 was to the north of Narvik, the main air attacks began.

The Sea Hurricanes were caught off balance. As had been planned, most of them were committed to attacking the shadowers and so, when waves of bombers attacked the ships, they were away chasing their elusive quarries through thick cloud, fruitlessly expending their ammunition against the heavily armoured Blohm und Voss 138's. There were three main attacks on the convoy. In the second and strongest of these over fifty bombers attacked, and a formation of thirty-seven torpedo aircraft broke through and sank eight ships. Only one aircraft, a Heinkel III, was destroyed by *Avenger*'s fighters.

On the following day the Luftwaffe returned in strength. Four massive attacks were made on PQ18 in the afternoon.

The Germans tried to disorganise and soften up the convoy and its escorts by high-level bombing attacks and by dropping mines from aircraft. Then the torpedo planes and dive-bombers attacked. The Heinkels came on in line abreast, flying in close formation only a few feet above the sea, then fanned out as they closed the ships for the drop. One attack was made by forty Ju 88's which swept in low on the convoy's starboard bow looking, one observer said, 'like a huge flight of nightmare locusts'. Above the Heinkels and Junkers flew squadrons of Me 109's.

But the Hurricanes had changed their tactics and reserved their main strength to fight off the attacking aircraft. The results were far more satisfactory.

One Hurricane pilot who, with his wingman, a Petty Officer, tackled fourteen Ju 88's flying in diamond formation, found them 'a pretty hard nut to crack, for if they can keep formation, their cross fire keeps every plane covered.

'However, I made a quarter attack on the leading plane, then swung away straight at one of the planes on the side of the diamond. At the last second I flicked underneath him; he got the wind up and pulled the nose of his plane hard up, and the Petty Officer, flying just on my starboard wing, gave him a lovely burst which put paid to his account. The formation broke up and there was a lovely scrap all over the sky.

'That sort of thing went on all day. As soon as we were out of ammunition or petrol, we dived down to the carrier, landed, re-armed and re-fuelled and took off again. My lunch was a gulp of cold tea. Our squadron made seventeen sorties that day.'

Twenty German aircraft were shot down in these attacks on the 13th by the Sea Hurricanes and the tremendously fierce barrage put up by the escorts and merchant ships. Only one merchantman was sunk, and of the three Hurricanes lost, two of the pilots were saved.

When they returned next day the Germans made a dead set at the *Avenger*, to try to eliminate the source of the fighter opposition. Waves of Junkers and Heinkels aimed bombs and torpedoes at her. Her fighters attacked them and spoiled their aim, and her Captain, Commander A. P. Colthurst, himself a very experienced torpedo bomber pilot, successfully dodged seventeen torpedo tracks making straight for the ship and brought her through unscathed. He made a signal to Admiral Burnett in *Scylla* claiming four enemy aircraft destroyed and three probables.

The torpedo bombers had been roughly handled by the *Avenger*'s remaining nine Hurricanes, and thereafter left the convoy alone. Three hours of high and low-level bombing attacks on the following day, the 14th, left the convoy un-harmed and the wreckage of a dozen more German aircraft littering the sea.

Shortly after this the main escort vessels, including the *Avenger*, left the convoy to join the homeward bound QP13. PQ18 was then under the protection of her normal close escort, a few Catalinas and Russian destroyers, and the Sea Hurricane of the *Empire Morn*.

At 1015 the RDF guard ship reported enemy aircraft near the convoy. Flying Officer A. H. Burr climbed into the cockpit of Hurricane V.7653 and made ready for launching. A number of Ju 88's appeared at about 4,000 feet and began making individual bombing and dive-bombing attacks on the ships from cloud. It was thought impractical to launch the Hurricane.

About 1100 it was reported that nine Heinkel III torpedo aircraft were coming in from astern low on the water. The Fighter Direction Officer,

Three views of the tanker Rapana. Top: *In her peacetime trim.*
Centre: *In wartime, just before conversion*
Bottom: *Newly converted into a Merchant Aircraft Carrier*

Lieutenant Carrique, gave instructions to launch, but the Captain saw that the ship was not clear ahead and warned the Catapult Directing Officer, Pilot Officer Davies, with his red flag. Then Burr found that his electrical system had broken down completely. With bombs from the Ju 88's falling round the ship, the catapult crew checked fuses and changed the battery.

At 1150 another group of torpedo planes was reported coming in from the port quarter of the convoy. This time the Hurricane got off, though as the *Empire Morn* was in a position in the centre of the convoy Burr had to swerve violently to avoid the balloon cables of the other ships. He also had to dodge Bofors and Oerlikon shells from some of the ships, which opened up on him.

He was in immediate communication with the FDO, and climbing to 700 feet flew round to the port quarter of the convoy where he saw below him fifteen Heinkels flying in line abreast fifty feet above the sea about three miles from the stern of the convoy. He immediately dived on them and made a head-on and a port beam attack on one machine, opening fire at three hundred yards and closing to a hundred and fifty. He saw his bullets hitting the nose and one of the engines, and as he turned above and behind the Heinkel to the left he noticed white smoke coming from its starboard engine. He closed in again to two hundred and fifty yards and used up the rest of his ammunition in beam attacks on the starboard side. White smoke poured from both the Heinkel's engines. Burr was now getting in the way of flak from the ships so he broke off and flew round the stern of the convoy to the starboard side.

From there he watched all the remaining Heinkels drop their torpedoes, and all miss their targets. Flying round the front of the convoy he saw the wreckage of his Heinkel in the water in between two columns of ships on the port side of the convoy. He decided to patrol the starboard side of the convoy, for, although he had used all his ammunition, 'it was,' as he put it, 'my intention to show myself to any other formation and endeavour to break it up with a mock attack.'

No more enemy aircraft appeared, though the original Ju 88's were still dropping bombs from the clouds. Burr checked his petrol and found that he had seventy gallons left. He asked the FDO for a distance and vector to the nearest Russian airfield. Carrique gave him Keg Ostrov 240 miles away on a vector of 180° Magnetic.

'I decided,' Burr wrote in his report, 'to try and save the aircraft and I set out on this course allowing 10° for drift, steering 170° M.'

'I ran into a fog bank about 40 miles wide after 15 minutes flying but managed to make a land-fall and pinpoint my position. I flew at heights between 200 and

2,000 feet and arriving at Archangel I fired the recognition signal and found Keg Ostrov aerodrome with 5 gallons in my reserve tank left.'

No warships had been sunk throughout the passage of PQ18 and it had come through with relatively fewer losses than any Russian convoy so far. Out of thirty-nine merchantmen, one rescue ship and one oiler, ten ships had been sunk by air attack, most of them when the *Avenger*'s Hurricanes had been off on their wild goose chase of the shadowers, and three by U-boats.

The barrage provided by the specially adapted anti-aircraft cruiser *Scylla*, the 'fighting destroyer escort', the close escort and the merchantmen themselves, accounted for thirty-five enemy aircraft, confirmed or probable. *Avenger*'s Hurricanes destroyed five German machines, with three probables and fourteen more damaged, for the loss of four Hurricanes, three of whose pilots were saved.

The carrier's three Swordfish had also been in action. Throughout the passage they flew anti-submarine patrols, sometimes in icing conditions at 500 feet. In these appalling conditions their half-frozen crews sighted several U-boats and attacked them with depth charges, forcing them to dive, and guiding the destroyers of the fighting escort to them. This co-operation produced at least one confirmed kill. The performance of these three Swordfish was significant for the future of the Merchant Aircraft Carriers, which would each be operating a tiny air group of Stringbags in these numbers with precisely the same role.

The *Avenger* was now wanted for the North African landings, as were the next escort carriers when they were ready. Coupled with the general shortage of escorts this resulted in a postponement of Russian convoys until the end of the year. Priority had to be given to the North Atlantic convoys, without which Britain would starve. Battles were raging there, with convoys suffering very heavy losses, some of them up to half their ships, especially in the 500-mile mid-ocean gap which aircraft could not cover until there were ships to take them there.

The Admiralty took advantage of the bad winter weather of 1942–43 and started sending convoys through again to Russia at Christmas. On December 30th *Lutzow*, *Hipper* and six destroyers attacked convoy JW51B, of fifteen ships escorted by five destroyers, two corvettes and a trawler, with Admiral Burnett's cruisers *Sheffield* and *Jamaica* covering them from a temporary base at Kola Inlet. The escort destroyers held off the *Hipper* until the arrival of Burnett who drove off the German force, sinking one destroyer. At the end of February, 1943, Russian convoys were stopped again, with the intention of renewing them in the following November.

8

In the last quarter of 1942, while so many auxiliary carriers lay on the stocks, and the first Merchant Aircraft Carriers were still in dockyard hands, great losses were suffered by both sides in the Battle of the Atlantic. Allied escorts were only sinking U-boats at about half the rate at which they were being produced; the Allies in fact were losing ships, cargoes and crews at an alarming rate. It was a race of attrition. With the extra need to protect the great mass of shipping backing up the North African landings, Operation 'Torch', escorts were spread much more thinly. The U-boats took full advantage of this, and in November they sank over 700,000 tons, the highest monthly figure of the whole war. In the four months from August to November over 2,000,000 tons had been sunk.

On November 1st a convoy was in position 43° North 15°24′ West, about 550 miles from Gibraltar when it picked up a shadowing FW 200. Flying Officer N. Taylor was launched from the CAM-ship *Empire Heath*. He shot down the Condor but his Hurricane was badly hit and he was nearly drowned.

With the convoys being decimated for want of air protection, in September, 1942, Sir Amos Eyre, Assistant Head of Admiralty Merchant Ship New Construction, gave his approval to the scheme for tanker Merchant Aircraft Carriers. The plan to convert the *Queens* into carriers was scrapped, mainly because the Allies could not afford to lose the huge troop-carrying capacities of these ships, which would be out of service about a year, particularly when large numbers of American troops were being brought across for the North African invasion. This was thought to outweigh the potential benefit of two or three super auxiliary carriers with hangar capacity for sixty to eighty wing-folded Swordfish and an endurance of 6,000 miles at 25 knots.

Detailed plans for the tanker conversions were prepared very quickly by John Lamb's Anglo-Saxon Petroleum staff and were speedily accepted, with a few modifications, by the Admiralty and Ministry of War Transport. In October,

1942, it was decided to convert six tankers, four of them under construction and two of them Anglo-Saxon ships already operating. At the same time the grain ship conversion programme was expanded from two to six ships. The tankers selected were larger than the grain ships, but the greater usefulness of their longer flight decks would be reduced because, unlike the grain ships, there would be no room for a hangar in their structure, and their aircraft would have to be stowed in a permanent deck park aft on the flight deck. Lack of a hangar also meant that they could only carry three instead of four Swordfish.

The gales of December, 1942, and January, 1943, reduced the German attacks on Allied convoys, but in February losses of Allied merchant ships began to rise again as the U-boats resumed the offensive. '. . . the Germans,' says the official Admiralty record, 'never came so near to disrupting communications between the New World and the Old as in the first twenty days of March 1943.' Forty-one ships were sunk in the first ten days, fifty-six in the second ten days, more than 500,000 tons, of which nearly two-thirds were sunk in convoy. 'It appeared possible', said the Naval Staff, 'that we should not be able to continue convoy as an effective system of defence.' But the sinking of U-boats was also at its peak. In March the Royal Navy escort carriers *Biter*, *Archer* and *Dasher*, and the US Navy's *Bogue*, joined the special anti-submarine Support Groups in the Western Approaches. In April the average monthly loss of U-boats was eighteen, almost matching the rate of building.

Luftwaffe anti-shipping aircraft now had to make wide detours to avoid Allied Beaufighters and Mosquitoes over the Bay of Biscay. After being temporarily switched to the Russian Front for transport duties, the Condors of *III Gruppe KG 40* resumed the offensive from Bordeaux-Merignac and Cognac in the spring of 1943. Routine reconnaissance patrols were now taken over by Junkers Ju 290A's of *FAGr* at Mont de Marsan, and *KG 40* Condors only took off armed with bombs when a definite target had been reported. The aircraft flew low and took it in turns to climb at intervals to 1,500 feet in a wide circle, carrying out a search with their *Hohentwiel* radar. The first aircraft crew to sight the target told the others by R/T. Low level attacks on shipping had been forbidden for a long time, and a minimum attacking altitude of 9,000 feet was laid down. With *Hohentwiel* radar, however, hits were scored reasonably often by blind bombing from these heights.

In April, 1943, the Merchant Aircraft Carriers, soon abbreviated to MAC-ships, too began to appear. They and the RN escort carriers were the final twin offspring of Captain Slattery's 'suitable merchant ships' with the 'simplest

Amastra *in peace and war.*   *Above, as a tanker . . .*

possible flight deck and landing equipment', and of the pioneer *Empire Audacity*.
From now on the Red Duster and the White Ensign would work together. With
the Merchant Carriers looking after the merchants, the escort carriers could go
to the special escort hunter-killer Support Groups, and be used as Fleet carriers
in their own right.

On April 14th the first MAC-ship, the grain ship *Empire MacAlpine*, owned
by W. Thompson of Leith, was commissioned. Cargo was carried in eight large
holds, filled through trunkways extending to the flight deck, where flush water-
tight hatch covers were fitted. The hangar was at the after end of the ship and
contained ample space for four Swordfish with folded wings, as well as all the
necessary spares. A hangar hoist was fitted with a platform 42 feet by 20 feet
for transporting the planes to the flight deck. The flight deck on the *Empire
MacAlpine* was 422 feet long and 62 feet in beam, with a minimum freeboard of
28 feet 6 inches at the fore end above the load waterline when the ship was in
service condition. One 4-inch gun, four 20-millimetre and two 40-millimetre
Oerlikons formed her gun armament.

All the Swordfish for the MAC-ships were drawn from No. 836 Squadron of
the Fleet Air Arm, formed originally by Lieutenant Commander R. W. Slater,
and based first at Belfast, then at RNAS Maydown, near Londonderry, on
Lough Foyle. In May 1943 Slater flew a Swordfish aboard the *Empire MacAlpine*,
the first time an aircraft had ever landed on a merchant ship. The *Empire
MacAlpine* sailed for Halifax with her first convoy on May 29th.

Now that the new small carriers were coming into service with the convoys the Merchant Ship Fighter Unit and the Fighter Catapult Ships were considered redundant. HQ Fighter Command sent the following message to HQ Number 9 Group:

'It is requested that you will forward to the Merchant Ship Fighter Unit the following message, which has been received from the Admiralty.

'"My Lords would like to express their great appreciation of the services rendered by the RAF in providing this valuable service for our convoys, and it is with great regret that we are now forced to recommend that this association of the RAF with the Merchant Navy should now be brought to an end."'

The order to disband the MSFU went out from HQ Fighter Command on June 8th. At that time there were five CAM-ships left in service. The last two of these were expected to return to the UK about July 6th.

The convoy containing the last two CAM-ships, *Empire Tide* and *Empire Darwin*, did not in fact leave Gibraltar until July 23rd. German Intelligence reported the disbandment of the MSFU and the enemy took advantage of what they thought was a convoy with no close air support.

On July 26th, when the convoy was between latitudes 43° and 45°, which was

. . . and, below, Amastra *as a tanker/aircraft carrier*

The return of B-for-Bertie—a Swordfish immediately after landing on a Merchant Aircraft Carrier

normally out of range of effective air cover from either Britain or Gibraltar, a Focke-Wulf 200 was sighted about twelve miles away. At 0847 on the 28th, when the convoy was on course due north, they picked up reports that a convoy had been bombed and more than one ship sunk about a hundred miles east of them.

At 1555 an unidentified aircraft was picked up thirty-five miles astern on RDF. At 1914 an unidentified aircraft fourteen miles to the south was reported by an escort ship. Then a United States Liberator was sighted dead ahead. The first aircraft was identified as a FW 200 and the Liberator was ordered to attack it. At 1921 a port engine of the Focke-Wulf burst into flames and it crashed. The Liberator had been vitally hit in the fight and also crashed.

At 1930 an enemy aircraft was reported twelve miles away at six o'clock. The machine, a Condor, appeared, flew round the port side of the ships towards the head of the convoy, then turned towards the sun. About 1937 Flying Officer J. A. Stewart was launched from the *Empire Darwin*, which was leading the starboard column of the convoy, after the ship had turned 15° to avoid the full pitching effect of the swell.

At 250 mph, 2,600 revs and 6¼ boost, Stewart gave chase, and the Fighter Direction Officer, Sub-Lieutenant Ward, heard his 'Tally-ho!' on the R/T almost at once. He made a quarter attack on the enemy in the teeth of heavy return fire, and a white flash was seen near the FW's turret, then both aircraft disappeared from the view of the *Empire Darwin* at a distance of about fifteen miles. The Condor crashed into the sea.

At 2036 Flying Officer P. J. R. Flynn, late of Number 124 (Baroda) Squadron, was launched from the *Empire Tide*, a veteran of Russian convoys, which led the port column, in the exceptionally good time of eighty-four seconds. The FDO, Sub-Lieutenant Pickwell, directed him on to a FW 200 which was flying across the convoy dead ahead at 150 mph, about twelve miles away.

Flynn climbed to about two hundred feet and at about 300 mph overhauled the FW in about two and a half minutes. He came in on the port quarter and opened up with a two-second burst at about three hundred yards. Return fire came in short bursts from the Condor's port side lateral machine-gun and from both turrets. Flynn's first burst looked slightly low to him, judging by the splashes in the sea.

He climbed into the sun and made a series of beam and quarter attacks from the port side, up sun. On his second run he concentrated mainly on the cockpit. Heavy return fire hit the Hurricane in the wings. On a third pass he sprayed the fuselage between the rear upper turret and the lateral gun position in the hope of reducing the return fire. He saw his bullets hitting all along the fuselage and cockpit. He also gave the front upper turret one short burst. This was at ranges between a hundred and two hundred yards.

Flynn made three more attacks. He hit one engine, and saw smoke pour from it but noticed no flames, which may have been swamped by the considerable glare from the sea. The Condor took no evasive action at all, but relied on

Ancylus

heavy machine-gun and cannon fire which holed the Hurricane's port wing badly and smashed the perspex behind Flynn's head. To his surprise Flynn saw a bomb fall in front of him, apparently aimed at the Hurricane. He felt the blast but nothing more. The FW released the rest of its bombs, some six or seven. As Flynn broke away, all his ammunition used up, he saw it losing height, smoke pouring from its inner port engine.

Flynn flew back towards the convoy, now about forty miles away and out of his R/T range. He climbed to about 3,000 feet and after about ten minutes sighted the ships. Still unable to get into R/T contact, owing to a blank patch, he flew on a steady course waggling his wings. He circled the convoy and was eventually instructed by the FDO to orbit at 10,000 feet. When he had reached between 5,000 and 6,000 feet he saw a FW 200 quite near him at about 12,000 feet. He was told to clear the line of fire of the ships' HAA. He told the FDO that he intended to bale out near one of the escort vessels. He abandoned the aircraft at 2,000 feet, hit the sea, inflated his dinghy and waited. After ten minutes he was on the point of hoisting his small sail when the escort, HMS *Enchantress*, appeared to pick him up. It was 2138, half an hour before dusk. *Enchantress'* whaler took just ten minutes to make the rescue, from lowering to re-hoisting. Twenty-three minutes before, Stewart had also been picked up, after firing a red light from the water.

Both pilots had performed excellently, particularly as it had been the first combat for both of them, Stewart having joined the MSFU straight from his Officers' Training Unit. As the swansong of the Merchant Ship Fighter Unit the action was magnificently appropriate. The escort carriers and MAC-ships had now taken over the duty of stopping the gap that yawned between coast-bound air patrols, a job which the expendable fighters of the CAM-ships and Fighter Catapult Ships had done so well. For two years there had been long periods when CAM-ship Hurricanes were the only air defence available to Allied convoys in the areas beyond land-based air coverage. The Luftwaffe had quickly learned to respect them, and the presence of one of them in a convoy was always a strong deterrent. It was the men of the MSFU who were largely responsible for removing the threat by the long-range FW 200 bombers, which had at one time seemed so serious. This was their great achievement.

Acavus entering port, Halifax, Nova Scotia

9

In July, 1943, the *Rapana*, the first Anglo-Saxon Company Merchant Aircraft Carrier, went into service, having only berthed at Smith's Dock in North Shields for conversion in February. The job had taken five months, about a third of the time needed to build an escort carrier. It was a great pity that the idea of the Merchant Aircraft Carrier had not been taken up much earlier and implemented with greater speed and imagination. Many men, ships and cargoes could have been saved. Now it seemed as if the MAC-ships had come too late. With the loss of forty-one U-boats in May of 1943, about a third of all U-boats at sea, Admiral Doenitz had for the time being conceded defeat. He withdrew all his submarines from the convoy routes.

The defeat, however, was unlikely to be final, and the MAC-ships would in any case make the job of the escort carriers lighter and allow the Admiralty to use them more flexibly.

In planning their MAC-ship conversions, the Anglo-Saxon Marine Technical Division team had calculated that an additional eight hundred tons weight would be added to a tanker by the conversion, mostly in the form of prefabricated steel structures. Lloyds added a further two hundred tons of strengthening. Part of the accommodation structure amidships, the navigating bridge, the upper superstructure aft, and a thirty-foot high funnel had all to be removed so that the flight deck would be low enough for structural solidarity and stability.

The all-welded steel flight deck, 460 feet long and 62 feet wide, was constructed in sections with telescopic joints to allow it to expand and contract freely as a result of temperature changes between the North Atlantic and the Caribbean and the flexing of the deck in a seaway. Arrester gear and a crash barrier were fitted, the hydraulic units controlling the arrester wires being housed on platforms level with the original fore-and-aft gangway. A catwalk was fitted round the perimeter of the flight deck for the safety of the aircraft maintenance and handling parties.

Horizontal funnels and a system similar to that used by some Fleet carriers for damping down the smoke and gases which might otherwise impede landing had also to be introduced in all MAC conversions. A new wheelhouse and navigation bridge, which also functioned as aircraft control platform and signal top, were built on the starboard side of the flight deck.

A complete petrol system was installed to ensure rapid fuelling of the aircraft. This comprised two large all-welded steel storage tanks built up in Number 3 centre cargo tank and a steam pumping unit installed in the after pump room with discharges at the forward and after ends of the flight deck. This meant a certain reduction in the cargo capacity.

The ship's electrical system was entirely renewed. The original steam and diesel generators were replaced by larger units to meet the increased electrical load, and two additional diesel generators were fitted.

Armament was increased. The merchantman's orthodox DEMS 4-inch gun was moved aft under the round-down of the flight deck, and steel sponsons built on either side of the flight deck to support two Bofors and six Oerlikons.

Additional deckhouses forward and aft of the original bridge superstructure were built for the Fleet Air Arm personnel, as well as enlarged galleys and bakeries and a naval type sick-bay complete with operating theatre. The crew's accommodation in the foc's'le was transferred to the poop space, and a new deckhouse built between poop and flight decks for engineer officers' accommodation and aircraft component storerooms. The foc's'le space and the fore hold were converted into magazines, workshops and storerooms.

The MAC-ship *Empire MacAndrew*, converted in Denny's yard, also went into service in July 1943, followed by the tanker conversion *Amastra*, another Smith's Dock job, and the grainer *Empire MacRae* from Lithgow's in September.

It had been thought that the MAC-ships might carry a fighter as well as their Swordfish, and Sub-Lieutenant Brown, the ex-*Audacity* pilot, proved that this could be done when he landed a Martlet aboard the *Amastra*. This was never followed up, largely because the threat from FW Condors diminished, though a fighter operating in co-operation with Swordfish would have been valuable in attacks on U-boats, as events showed.

The new MAC-ships were completed in time for a renewed offensive by the U-boats, armed with new weapons and methods. British radar, both in ships and aircraft, had become very efficient in locating U-boats travelling on the surface, and aircraft and ships had been beating the U-boats in battle. Submarines had to surface to re-charge their batteries and travel on the surface to

Top: *Landing*
Centre: *One of the escorts*
Bottom: *Heavy landing*

reach their hunting grounds quickly enough, so the U-boats had already begun to carry heavier gun armament to fight off attacking aircraft on the surface. These now became standard tactics. The Germans were also trying hard to invent a search-receiver which could pick up Allied radar transmission without betraying its own presence. But the weapon at the heart of the new U-boat offensive was the acoustic torpedo. This was a torpedo which homed on the noise of a ship's propellers. It was at its most efficient against ships steaming at medium speeds, and was aimed mainly at the convoy escorts.

The new offensive began with attacks against a combination of two Allied convoys, ONS18 and ON22, sixty-six merchant ships and seventeen escorts, in September. The combined convoys had close air support, but thick foggy weather made flying very difficult. Included in ONS18 was the first of the Merchant Aircraft Carriers to see service, *Empire MacAlpine*, with three Swordfish aboard.

Flying conditions were too bad until the afternoon of September 21st, by which time the U-boats had already begun their attacks. Then the fog lifted and the Senior Officer Escort asked *Empire MacAlpine* for a patrol astern of the convoy. A Swordfish piloted by Sub-Lieutenant R. A. Singleton, with Lieutenant Commander J. Palmer as observer, took off. Ten minutes later the convoy was again enveloped in thick fog.

The Swordfish carried out its allotted patrol but they sighted nothing hostile. They were on their return flight when Palmer got a contact on his ASV radar set. They closed the contact and found it to be the corvette K164 which asked them for the position of the convoy. Palmer calculated the bearing and distance of the ships by ASV observation and passed them to the corvette.

The Swordfish approached the convoy through the dense fog, blind except for its own radar and the 251M set in the *Empire MacAlpine*, which homed the Swordfish to the position of the carrier, invisible as it was to the airmen. The men in the MAC-ship heard the Swordfish approaching from astern. Aldis lamps were turned on to guide them in. Then it passed directly over the ship, so accurate had been both radar operators, and so unusually free from error their sets. But the aircraft was not down, and the ship lay hidden in fog. Singleton flew on ahead to see if there were any breaks in the fog. But it stretched ahead unbroken. With petrol running low, there was nothing for it but to make a pass at the deck.

Fortunately the wind was about 15° on the port bow, so no radical alteration of course was called for by the ship. Using his radar to avoid the ships all around him, Captain W. F. Riddell, Master of the *Empire MacAlpine*, steered the ship carefully to leeward so as to give Singleton as good an approach as possible. The Swordfish circled the ship above the fog to try to make sure that there was nothing astern to interfere with the approach. Riddell turned the ship into wind, gave the affirmative by signal lamp and R/T, and streamed a fog buoy, which the pilot used as a guide.

With visibility about a hundred yards, Singleton made his approach. The batsman, using lighted bats, waved him off. He approached again, with his forward view now down to about fifty yards, and this time made a perfect landing.

A second Swordfish patrol was carried out later that day from *Empire MacAlpine* in conditions of ten-tenths cloud at 700 feet, with visibility about seven miles. Two searches to a depth of ten miles were ordered by R/T when the Swordfish was airborne and carried out, but the only vessels sighted were a merchantman which had been torpedoed overnight and other ships steaming to her rescue. On one of the searches contact was made on R/T with a shore-based aircraft.

A third patrol was as unproductive as the second. At 1305 a report was received of a suspected U-boat bearing 230°, forty miles from the convoy. At 1310 a Swordfish took off and set course to intercept, with ten-tenths cloud at 1,200 feet and a cold grey ocean below. Nothing was sighted on that bearing and at 1343 the Swordfish turned back to find the convoy. Two minutes later they were called up by the SO Escort and ordered to search on a bearing 050° for thirty miles. They sighted nothing and once more set course to close the convoy. On returning to the convoy they were ordered to make another patrol to port. A whale was sighted during this search, and very nearly attacked.

Patrol 5 of the day, carried out at 1,000 feet under ten-tenths cloud was uneventful. The weather was getting thicker again when the ship got a report of a U-boat inside the convoy. A Swordfish took off and flew low between the columns of ships, with cloud base less than a hundred feet and visibility under a quarter of a mile. Nothing hostile was seen. SO Escort wanted the Swordfish to extend the search but fog was now enveloping the convoy again and the aircraft was brought in. One more search was flown that day ahead of the convoy but the aircraft reported the weather there even worse and was ordered to return.

By the afternoon of the following day, September 22nd, the fog had cleared away. At 1641 Swordfish B (HS381), pilot Sub-Lieutenant B. I. Barlow, observer Sub-Lieutenant J. Boyd, took off from *Empire MacAlpine* armed with two depth-charges. The sky was clear up to 20,000 feet and they could see for twenty miles over a smooth, shining sea. The climbing biplane was silhouetted against the

Pilot's eye view

*And that of the observer . . .
. . . the carrier whose aircraft
has just left*

sunset. At 1818, when they had been flying over an apparently empty ocean for just over an hour and a half and were at a point in their search pattern about eight miles from the convoy, they sighted a U-boat making a good 18 knots on the surface.

The Swordfish remained at 3,000 feet and Boyd sent a first sighting and position report by R/T. The U-boat was a small 517-ton type, steering 220°. Barlow climbed to 4,000 feet and circled the U-boat, waiting for a reply from the *Empire MacAlpine*.

Boyd was getting nothing on his receiver. The situation was difficult for the Swordfish. Now that U-boats went heavily armed against aircraft, an attack by a lone Stringbag was bad tactics. The Swordfish crew knew it, and so, obviously, did the captain of the U-boat, which had made no attempt to dive but was weaving about below in evasive action. But if the Swordfish received no instructions soon they would have to attack. After about five minutes of this Boyd called for assistance, but the set was dead.

They continued circling and reported the submarine's alteration of course to 160°. Then they sighted an escort vessel and circled her, Boyd flashing details of the U-boat to her. She acknowledged. Boyd reported the U-boat still on the surface. Then they saw the submarine alter course again. Boyd tried the R/T again. She was now on course 090°, closing the convoy at full speed. Then he flashed the bearing of the enemy to the escort. A few minutes after this they saw another Swordfish approaching.

This was Swordfish C (LS281), from *Empire MacAlpine*, pilot Sub-Lieutenant P. T. Gifford, observer Lieutenant J. H. G. Tapscott. Boyd's signals had reached the convoy, and Swordfish C had taken off at 1823, armed with four

The new broom . . .

rocket projectiles. They flew at 2,000 feet, steering slightly to the west of the course they had been given so as to arrive up-sun of their target.

At 1840, shortly after sunset, they sighted the U-boat five miles on their port beam, heading 230° at about 18 knots. They closed to within two miles of her, making S-turns up-sun while Tapscott reported the sighting. When Swordfish B sighted the R/P Swordfish she began to climb to 5,000 feet to attack with her depth-charges.

At 1843 Swordfish C closed the range to 2,000 yards and dived down-sun from the U-boat's starboard beam. The U-boat crew were either taken by surprise or deliberately held their fire until the Swordfish was about 1,400 yards away. The submarine took no evasive action. At about 1,200 to 1,300 yards the Swordfish fired her first pair of rockets.

They were correct for line, Tapscott judged, but about a hundred feet short. The U-boat had now opened a fairly heavy barrage from a large-calibre gun on the for'ard deck and smaller ones fore and aft on the conning tower and after deck. At eight hundred yards Gifford fired their second ripple. These went over the target. Boyd in Swordfish B estimated that each ripple had missed by sixty feet on either side of the U-boat.

Swordfish C then turned to port to make her getaway. When they straightened out Tapscott saw shell bursts falling two hundred yards short of them and to port. Almost at once the German gunners corrected for aim, line and fuse setting. White bursts from multiple gun mountings, black bursts from a heavier gun with a slower rate of fire, rocked the Swordfish. There was a heavy concentration of guns around and immediately in front of the conning-tower and on the after deck.

. . . Rapana *immediately after conversion*

Swordfish B dived from 5,000 feet to make her depth-charge attack. At 4,000 feet the intense anti-aircraft fire from the U-boat made them break off and climb to 9,000 feet. Going down to 5,500 feet they dive-bombed the submarine through the barrage. At 6,000 feet shells were bursting two hundred yards away.

Their depth-charges fell about two hundred yards wide and only one exploded. But the U-boat was now heading away from the convoy, on course 090° at full speed. They left the scene at 1917, with the nearest escort five miles from the U-boat, and set course for the *Empire MacAlpine*. They were brought in by radar at 1925, one hour and seven minutes after sunset.

The whole battle for these two convoys was fought over four days. Only six of the sixty-six merchantmen were sunk, but three escorts were destroyed by the new acoustic torpedoes and another badly damaged. Only two U-boats were sunk. It was a victory for the enemy, and the fog.

This was the first action for the untried Merchant Swordfish, and there was much room for improvement in their tactics. The two Swordfish might have been more successful against the heavily armed U-boat had they attacked together, though depth-charges were of limited use against a surfaced submarine in clear weather. When the convoy reached Halifax experiments were carried out with two aircraft, both armed with R/P's, attacking simultaneously.

What was really needed was the pairing off of a fighter with a Swordfish for a combined attack on a U-boat. These tactics had been used by escort carriers. The fighter attacked first and knocked out or reduced the U-boat's powerful gun-armament, clearing the way for the Swordfish to attack without hindrance. Unfortunately, although a Martlet had been successfully tested aboard a MAC-ship, fighters were never allotted to them for operations.

Of the achievement in bringing Singleton's Swordfish safely back to the deck on the 21st, Sir Max Horton, Admiral Commanding Western Approaches, wrote to the Admiralty, 'The homing and deck-landing of the Swordfish in Patrol 1 reflects the greatest credit on all concerned in view of the dense fog conditions prevailing . . .' The SO Escort called it '. . . one of the most amazing landings I have ever heard of . . .' The recovery of an aircraft in such foul conditions would have been considered exceptional for a big Fleet carrier. To bring a machine safely back to a deck only 390 feet long in thick fog was a phenomenal achievement. The vital part played by radar suggested its regular use in 'blind' landings.

10

As a victory the battle of ONS18 was a flash in the pan for the Germans. Fog did not fall again to camouflage the U-boats, and Allied air coverage was increased by an agreement with Portugal to operate aircraft from the Azores. Long-range aircraft from these bases could now cover the whole North Atlantic. They often co-operated with planes from an escort carrier, with the ship acting as control. On December 28th, 1943, a patrolling Sunderland attacked and forced down a FW 200C-6, which had been one of four FW's from Bordeaux-Merignac searching for British naval units. The Condor was carrying two of the new Henschel Hs 293A missiles. Eight FW 200C-8's were specially built as Hs 293A carriers and completed in January–February, 1944, but the weapon was not used in effective numbers, and in the autumn of 1944 the Germans lost their Biscay airfields.

To counter the acoustic torpedo Allied escorts towed an apparatus called a 'foxer', which made a noise similar to a ship's screws and fooled the torpedo. The only further victims were a Polish destroyer in October and two frigates and a corvette early in 1944.

The Merchant Stringbags did not see any more U-boats for a time, but went about their plodding, tiring and often hazardous patrols. For the Naval airmen and the merchant seamen, getting used to each other needed tact and tolerance, as their CAM-ship predecessors had discovered.

For the Swordfish crews each voyage really started at Royal Naval Air Station Maydown. There were several airfields on Lough Foyle, including Maydown, Eglington, Ballykelly and Limavady. Maydown was the nearest to Londonderry, being three miles out of town on the Eglington road. Living quarters were the familiar collection of Nissen huts on a rather sad, damp little green patch, with a mess and a bar in a big T-shaped Nissen. There was the usual parade ground with flagpole and whitewashed ropes, and two Soccer pitches. Aircrew were at liberty when flying ceased for the day, and a run ashore meant the local bus to Eglington or Derry, or as far as Portrush, Belfast or County Down on a forty-eight. There were week-end jaunts across the border to Strabane, where food was unrationed. The Padre ran weekly record recitals of classical music. A foundation stone of RNAS Maydown was Lieutenant Andrews, very tall, very thin, with steel-rimmed glasses, white hair and a knife-edged, querulous Ulster accent, to whom airmen took any query about accommodation.

To join a ship the Swordfish took off together and flew along Lough Foyle, east along the coast to Rathlin Island, then north-east up the Clyde, where the little carrier would be steaming, waiting for them to land on. Once down on the deck, out of the capacious rear cockpits would come kitbags and green Pusser's suitcases, and all the assorted baggage of the aircrews, pilots, observers and usually telegraphist-air-gunners.

Although under the immediate orders of the ship's Air Staff Officer, a lieutenant commander RN or RNVR, to bring them under the general command of the ship's master all the airmen had to sign the ship's articles. They received a shilling a month and a bottle of beer a day. Ratings signed on as deckhands, and officers acquired the dual rank of Merchant and Royal Navy officers. It was customary to wear the Merchant Navy badge in the lapels of their Naval uniforms. To any outraged senior officers attempting to suppress this apparent breach of King's Regulations and Admiralty Instructions it was firmly, and proudly, made clear that the wearers were fully entitled.

It was in this spirit that, as soon as they took over new Swordfish, many MAC-ship flights painted out the word ROYAL in ROYAL NAVY on the fuselage side near the tail and substituted MERCHANT. The Swordfish

Tanker/carrier Empire MacColl

were painted in Atlantic camouflage, mottled green-grey upper surfaces with white fuselage sides, and the legend MERCHANT NAVY in stark black letters on their white flanks was very positive. Merchant Aircraft Carriers flew the Red Ensign, and their movements were reported in Lloyds Shipping Register.

For a pilot or observer life on board centred upon cabin, saloon, lounge, chartroom and flight deck—they had to get used to Merchant Navy terminology. The Air Staff Officer had a cabin to himself, pilots and observers usually shared a cabin. A cabin had two bunks, sometimes one above the other, a small wardrobe, two chairs, two chests of drawers, one port-hole. The batsman sometimes shared a cabin with one of the ship's officers, but sometimes was lucky enough to get a double all to himself. The cabins usually opened on the same companionway, with an adjacent washroom. In some ships the cabins were aft, the saloon amidships, the lounge in the fo'c'sle, and progress between them in heavy weather could be perilous. The saloon was a severely functional room with two or three tables. The Master, Medical Officer, Chief Engineer, First Officer and Air Staff Officer ate together. In some ships MN and FAA officers sat together, in others they were segregated, though this was not usually by their own choice. They usually sat where the steward put them.

The atmosphere was usually very informal. Aboard ship, and often ashore, FAA officers wore civilian clothes, and even in the air the only concession to Royal Navy dress was probably an undress blue battledress top with bars of rank and wings. This was only to avoid being shot as armed non-combatants in the event of capture. It might be worn with a coloured shirt, grey trousers and suede shoes.

The lounge often occupied the full breadth of the bows and was a rather shallow compartment, lined with comfortable cushioned settees. Certain ships had a bar there, though it was more usual practice for the Chief Steward to ask all officers at the start of every trip what they wanted in the way of spirits, beer and tobacco, which would be delivered to their cabins. Small social gatherings often began in someone's cabin, grew, and spilled over for'ard into the lounge.

On some ships pilots and observers were given a non-flying duty, such as Armament, Radar, Signals or Meteorological Officer. One observer who volunteered for the latter and found himself translating coded messages from Whitehall and Washington into isobars, thoroughly irritated the SO Escort by referring in his first amateur forecast to a wind 'veering and backing'.

Alexia *before* . . .

Harmony between MN and FAA depended to a great extent on the Air Staff Officer. Some helped to boost morale by arranging various communal activities. There would be a deck-hockey championship, Signals versus Armament, seamen versus aircrew, etc., with a trophy made by the engineers; quizzes, brains trusts and ship's concerts. In *Empire MacAlpine* Sub-Lieutenant Geoffrey Banks, an observer, broadcast short stories at night and ran the occasional ITMA-type show, called 'Mid-Atlantic Merry-Go-Round' over the ship's tannoy. He and Sub-Lieutenant Terence Longdon, who wanted to be an actor after the war, performed comedy scenes from Shakespeare. A great favourite, at least with the performers, was the drinking scene from 'Twelfth Night', with the Chief Engineer invariably cast as Maria. The alcohol used was genuine and produced an early type of 'method' acting. In another ship all the flying personnel were classical music fans and there were daily record concerts in one or other of their cabins. In *Adula* long and keen poker sessions filled off-duty hours, especially that rather vicious variation of the game called Anaconda, for some time until it was realised that, on paper at least, hundreds of pounds were owed. The score sheet was then thrown overboard.

It was a case of making their own amusements, otherwise off-duty was one long round of drinking, card playing and desultory chat, especially when filthy weather prevented flying for several days. In one ship an atmosphere which was being poisoned by an embittered, morose, solitary Air Staff Officer was transformed when he was replaced by a merry, outgoing RN officer, who raised morale by simply exhuding *bonhommie*. Although it was rare for a ship's officer to join in the cabin gatherings, FAA and MN played darts and bridge and deck hockey together and maintained at least a superficial camaraderie.

Aircrews were briefed for a patrol by the ASO in the small chartroom immediately beneath the bridge island. Other than at briefing times its doors always seemed to be wide open, and it was the draughtiest room in the ship. Here they were given details of area of patrol, visibility, estimated speed and direction of wind, recognition signal of the day, and would be told their Track To Make Good (TMG), with alterations of course needed to complete their search pattern. Meanwhile, out in the dark and cold on the heaving, tilted flight deck, the maintenance ratings checked aircraft and armaments, removed covers and lashings, and ran up and tested engines.

Manning a revving Swordfish on a wet, windswept flight deck in a grey dawn required effort. Scaling the high flank of a Stringbag, jamming the blunt toes of flying boots into the numerous steps with their springloaded metal lids and heaving your swaddled bulk upwards and over was always a bit like negotiating the Knight's Climb at Cheddar Gorge, and in bad weather more like clawing up the Matterhorn, especially for the poor observer, loaded with chart, chartboard with rotatable protractors, pencils, dividers, rubbers, course and speed calculator, and, last but not least, the famous 'Souplate' or Wilkinson Computer, without which navigating a Stringbag became an even more inexact science than with.

A MAC-ship's normal position in her convoy was in the middle of the centre column, and to fly off aircraft she would have to head into wind. If the prevailing wind were only a point or two off the bow, the aircraft could get off the deck quickly—it was possible for three Swordfish to take off in under a minute— without the carrier leaving her position in the convoy. But if the wind blew abeam or worse still from astern, the MAC-ship had to drop astern clear of the

. . . and Alexia *after*

convoy and either steer 90° from the convoy or on an opposite course. At this time the carrier was very vulnerable to U-boats, and flying-off was a doubly tense experience.

For most of their period in service MAC-ships used the Mark II Swordfish, which had three open cockpits for pilot, observer and telegraphist-air-gunner. The latter sat facing the tail with the radio in front of him and a Vickers gas-operated machine-gun mounted aft of that. He braced his back against the bulkhead of the observer's cockpit for take-off and landing. The observer's seat was central, a backless round stool which could be collapsed forward on to the cockpit floor. He sat facing forward while navigating, but was recommended to face the tail and brace his back against the aft bulkhead of the pilot's cockpit for take-off and landing. The pilot's seat was much higher than the observer's, who could only see the top of his helmet when airborne.

Of the three, the 'O-type' was the most cramped, the most put-upon. As the cockpit was open, his parachute was attached to a metal ring in the deck by a 'G-string'. The presence of this, plus the bulky radar set on the starboard side of the cockpit, and the collapsible stool, severely hampered movement. There was no plotting table, the wretched observer being expected to hold his chart-board on his knees. In these conditions he was expected to carry out accurate Dead Reckoning navigation, which entailed a good deal of leaping up and down for wind findings and taking compass bearings. A practical 'O' got his fitter to put clamps or hooks on the for'ard bulkhead so that the chartboard could be held permanently stable during patrols. Early humiliating experiences of grovelling around on the cockpit floor for dropped pencils probably taught him to stow all such articles in a leather holdall similarly clamped, and to hang up the two computers in canvas bags.

In 1943 the Mark III Swordfish appeared and was subsequently issued to 836 Squadron. This was the final production version of the Stringbag. A new fitting was a radome containing an ASV Mark X scanner between the under-carriage legs. The telegraphist-air-gunners were dispensed with, and the observer's rickety camp stool was replaced by a bucket seat.

When weather permitted—and in the North Atlantic it more often did not—regular dawn and dusk patrols were flown, sometimes round but mainly ahead of the convoy to a depth of about sixty miles or the limit of visibility. If U-boats were reported searches were carried out over the suspected area at the request of the SO Escort. If more than one MAC-ship accompanied a convoy a duty rota was worked. The 'duty' ship supplied routine patrols or searches, the

Fairey Swordfish landing on the MAC-ship Empire MacKay, *off Nova Scotia, 1944*

Fairey Swordfish on the after lift of **Empire MacAndrew**

'stand-by' ship a strike, if called for, over a twelve-hour period. A third MAC-ship would be at 'stand-down'. All aircraft were of course to be available for a 'rat-hunt' if necessary.

A Swordfish normally patrolled one of four triangles, to cover which it would

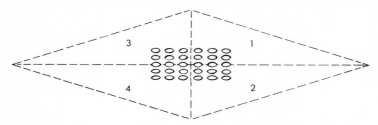

be given, say, a TMG of 090° for 60 miles, then 215° for 40 miles, then return to the carrier. Many observers mistrusted their radar sets, used them as little as possible, and relied on Dead Reckoning navigation.

An observer would first draw on his chart the Mean Line of Advance (MLA) of the convoy, then the first TMG. Using the estimated wind supplied by briefing, he worked out on his course and speed calculator the first course required, but as soon after take-off as possible he calculated the true wind and readjusted his course if necessary.

'Finding a wind' was a familiar ritual, as not only did winds in the Atlantic vary considerably, especially at different heights, but the ultimate destination of three men was a moving speck on a vast ocean. A good observer found a wind every twenty minutes or half an hour, other factors permitting.

On the observer's order 'Stand by to bomb . . . Bomb!' the observer started his stop-watch and the pilot released a smoke bomb. After waiting the necessary number of seconds to allow for the trajectory of the bomb, the observer ordered 'Stand by to turn! . . . Turn!' The pilot began a Rate 2 turn of 180°, which took exactly thirty seconds. The observer stopped and re-started his stop-watch. After one and a half minutes he repeated 'Stand by to turn! . . . Turn!' and the pilot started another Rate 2 turn in the same direction as before. The observer lined up the appropriate aircraft compass (of which there was one on each side of the cockpit) for a beam bearing and then noted down the exact time when the smoke plume appeared at 90°. He then lined up the compass for a quarter bearing and noted down the exact time when the smoke plume was at 135°. He applied these data plus the course and speed of the aircraft to the Wilkinson 'Souplate', which produced the exact speed and direction of the wind. He then plotted and calculated any alteration of aircraft course, using the new, true, wind to achieve the required TMG.

On the homeward leg of the triangle the observer had to allow for the MLA and speed of the convoy when calculating the final course to steer and the Estimated Time of Arrival. It was on this leg that most observers would make use of their radar, especially if visibility was bad. The ASV Mark I, with its simple linear scan, was not very effective for U-boat detection but effective at limited range as a check on position, because a convoy registered as a large echo on the screen. The manufacturers had optimistically calibrated it from 0 to 60 miles, but its true range varied with the height of the aircraft, and cautious observers were reluctant to use it beyond about thirty miles. It was certainly unwise to rely on it utterly, as it often failed to work properly. ASV Mark II, with its rotating scanner, was better, but in the view of many aircrew did not exceed the efficiency of three pairs of eyes for submarine hunting. On the other hand, some observers used it exclusively for navigating. The use of a MAC-ship's own radar in homing an aircraft, as the *Empire MacAlpine*'s had guided Singleton's Swordfish home, was rare. There are several cases on record of MAC Swordfish, caught airborne by sudden fog, being quite unable to locate their carriers for a landing, although directly over the convoy.

An aircraft could, in emergency only, request a radio bearing from the ship, but those who did were not popular with their ASO's. Strict radio silence was maintained to avoid helping the enemy to locate the convoy, except for a routine signal in Morse made at regular intervals (possibly once during each leg of the patrol triangle) by the telegraphist-air-gunner. R/T range at 1,000 or 2,000 feet, the normal operating height of a patrolling Swordfish, was not good but sufficient for normal patrols, which only took an aircraft from fifty to sixty miles from the ship.

All three crew members had headphones, but the TAG interpreted all messages before passing them on to the observer. With R/T the observer could hear a message but was more often than not too preoccupied with navigation to give it close attention. Most inter-communication in the aircraft was by shouting down Gosport speaking tubes. The issue of throat microphones for inter-

MAC-ship men
Top left: *Third Officer*, Empire MacRae. Top right: *Sub-Lieutenant Terence Longdon, who served both as pilot and observer*. Bottom left: *Sub-Lieutenant Geoffrey Banks (observer) with Sub-Lieutenant 'Bats' Hassington (right) on the bridge of* Empire MacKendrick. Bottom right: *Captain Collins of* Empire MacRae

communication by R/T was cause for great joy. Sometimes the TAG had to thump his observer, if the latter had temporarily unplugged while taking bearings, to attract his attention. Some observers liked the TAG to write down all signals first. They did not bother the pilot with routine messages.

On successfully locating the ship and landing on, a crew's greatest need was for hot food and drink. In the Anglo-Saxon Company's *Adula* this was often provided by the ship's Medical Officer, 'Doc' Moffatt. Lord Kilbracken, then Lieutenant J. R. Godley, RNVR, CO of *Adula*'s P-Flight, explains, 'The Merchant Navy officers and men were all members of a trade union, which laid down the exact hours they were to work; most men, even in wartime, even at sea, even in the face of the enemy, would not work a minute overtime. The stewards' working day began at seven-thirty in the morning, when they brought a cup of tea to each officer in his cabin, breakfast was at eight, and not a moment sooner; the last meal of the day was at six in the evening. So, if we were taking off on an early flight . . . we could get nothing to eat beforehand, and would be flying on extremely empty bellies, unless we cooked it ourselves, and, on return, we would still have half an hour to wait for breakfast. We therefore took care to bring good supplies on board with us: and Doc, who was just out of Bart's, and who had little work to do of a strictly professional kind, volunteered as cook, an office which he performed admirably.'

On another occasion, when *Adula*'s wooden ready-use stowages for rocket-projectiles had been smashed by heavy seas, Lieutenant Godley, knowing that a dawn patrol, and possibly searches or strikes, would almost certainly have to be flown on the following morning, asked the ship's carpenter to run up some new stowages as a matter of urgency. Chippy's reply was, 'I'll be glad to do them for you tomorrow, but today's Sunday.'

On a normal round voyage an aircrew would log between forty and fifty hours of flying. An average run to Halifax took about seventeen days, though a slow, four-knot convoy which struck bad weather could take as much as six weeks. About a hundred miles from the Canadian coast the MAC Swordfish would fly off to Dartmouth, near Halifax, and fill in the time before the return trip with flying practice and repairs. Ratings would often spend a few days leave at Halifax in private homes, thanks to the kindness of the Ajax Hospitality Club, which also distributed gifts at Christmas, and there was a regular flow of comforts, games and records from the Canadian Red Cross and the Navy League of Canada, which presented special Christmas 'ditty boxes'.

Three more MAC-ships, the tankers *Ancylus* and *Acavus* from the Anglo-Saxon Company fleet, and the *Empire MacKay*, came into service in October 1943. Eight Merchant Aircraft Carriers were now operational.

At dawn on October 8th, when the *Rapana* was at sea with convoy SC143, a U-boat was reported shadowing the convoy astern. This looked like the spotter for a wolf pack, and *Rapana* prepared to fly off a search. The first Swordfish crashed on take-off, though the crew were unhurt. A second U-boat attacked the convoy from the starboard bow and sank the merchantmen *Pendant III* and *Yorkman*, leaving only half a dozen survivors struggling in the water. *Rapana*'s aircraft made several attacks on U-boats sighted after that and claimed one damaged. Two U-boats were reported sunk by the convoy escorts.

In November the tanker *Empire MacColl* joined the MAC fleet. She was a new ship which had been converted while building at Cammell Laird's. Her Master, Captain E. J. Goodchild, had previously commanded the tanker *British Promise*, which had managed to make Halifax after two torpedoes had torn a gigantic hole in her side. *Empire MacColl* was one of three tankers of the British Petroleum Company to be converted into MAC-ships, and the Captain felt a little proud to be chosen out of about a hundred and fifty masters to command one.

His first 'lesson' was an interview with a Naval commander at Fanem House, who told him the origins and purpose of Merchant Aircraft Carriers. Then he went on various courses to learn the craft of commanding an aircraft carrier. At an early stage he met the Air Staff Officer of *Empire MacColl*, and they were together for about a month. They flew to Maydown, where they stayed for nearly a week. Here they attended lectures with FAA pilots and observers and went out in a Lockheed Hudson of Coastal Command to meet an incoming convoy. After this they spent some days aboard the old carrier *Argus* in the Clyde, operating between Arran and Ardrossan when Captain Fancourt instructed Goodchild in the art of manoeuvring for despatching and landing

*Fairey Swordfish **Mark III** showing the ASV scanner below the fuselage and, behind this, the **Rocket Assisted** Take Off Gear (RATOG)*

aircraft. The following week was spent at Derby House in Liverpool on the anti-submarine course, then, about the middle of October, Goodchild joined the *Empire MacColl* at Birkenhead, and the senior members of the ship's staff began to arrive. In the meantime the Chief Engineer, Chief Electrician, and others had attended courses on fire-fighting and arrester gear management. Towards the end of November they left the Mersey for the Clyde and trials started.

Their three Swordfish flew over from Maydown and landed aboard and they had their first practice take-offs and landings. By this time the ship was no longer strange to Captain Goodchild, as he had been in a carrier atmosphere for some months. By the middle of December they were ready to be operational, and sailed with their first convoy on December 15th.

Captain Goodchild disproved the rumour that MAC-ships were hard to handle. 'The *Empire MacColl*,' he recalled later, 'handled beautifully. Indeed she was a great deal better than what we used to call "Woolworth carriers"—which were a cross between MAC-ships and Fleet carriers. They were very light, and could be very difficult. In the case of the *Empire MacColl* I never used to have her fully loaded. With a draft of twenty-five feet, she behaved perfectly. I have even known the Swordfish to be able to land and take off in a gale.'

In December the grain ships *Empire MacCallum*, converted by Lithgow's, and *Empire MacKendrick*, a Burntisland conversion, and the tankers *Empire MacMahon* (Swan Hunter), *Empire MacCabe* (Swan Hunter) and *Alexia* went into service. The addition of the tankers *Medula* and *Adula* in January and February, 1944, brought the total of operational Merchant Aircraft Carriers to sixteen, which meant that at least one could normally be provided for each North Atlantic convoy, thus releasing escort carriers for work with the special escort groups.

In March 1944 the grainer *Empire MacDermott*, converted by Denny's, and the tanker *Gadila* from Smith's Dock became operational MAC-ships. Aircrews for the *Gadila* and the MAC-ship *Macoma*, commissioned later, were drawn from the Royal Netherlands Navy, and a separate squadron, No. 860, was formed to provide them. In March and April tanker MAC-ships were used to ferry aircraft from New York to Britain for use in Operation 'Overlord', the invasion of Normandy. In eleven voyages 212 aircraft were brought over.

The U-boat had declined as a result of the greater availability of anti-submarine aircraft and the successful antidote to the acoustic torpedo. However, in the spring of 1944 they began to get frisky again.

Convoy ON237, which included the MAC-ships *Empire MacKendrick* and *Ancylus*, sailed from Britain on May 19th, with M-Flight of 836 Squadron embarked in *Empire MacKendrick* and G-Flight in *Ancylus*.

In mid-afternoon on May 25th the convoy picked up HF/DF signals from

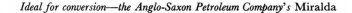

Ideal for conversion—the Anglo-Saxon Petroleum Company's Miralda

U-boats. Swordfish M2, pilot Sub-Lieutenant D. Shaw, observer Sub-Lieutenant H. W. M. Hodges, telegraphist-air-gunner Leading Airman J. M. King, took off from *Empire MacKendrick*. Aircraft G1, pilot Lieutenant O. C. Johnstone, observer Sub-Lieutenant J. K. G. Taylor, telegraphist-air-gunner Leading Airman J. Buckland, and aircraft G2, pilot Sub-Lieutenant B. J. Cooper, observer Sub-Lieutenant W. M. Owen, TAG Leading Airman F. J. Turner, went up from *Ancylus*. Six-tenths cloud at 5,000 feet obscured the sun, but visibility was about twenty miles. There was a ten-knot breeze blowing from 010°.

As they flew down the bearing 064°, on the track of the HF/DF signals, much of the cloud cleared away and the sun came through. At 1505 the two *Ancylus* Swordfish were steering 059° to make good their track, height about 4,000 feet, when Taylor, the observer of G1, and Cooper, piloting G3, both sighted the wake of a U-boat eight miles ahead, bearing Red 10° from them. The submarine was on the surface steering 055°, making at least 15 knots. Taylor sent the first sighting report, and the aircraft climbed and continued to close the U-boat. Two minutes after this sighting, the crew of Swordfish M2 saw the U-boat, which had now altered course to 080° and increased speed to about 18 knots. When M2 had closed to six miles the submarine made several turns to port and starboard, then swung back to 080°.

At 1510 intensive flak was bursting beneath G1 and G2, which made a slight alteration of course to starboard, then circled to port in line astern to try and take up a position ahead of the U-boat, which at 1513 also started to turn to port. Another two minutes, and they saw M2 closing in to attack from the U-boat's port beam. G1 and G2 immediately dived to make their own attack in co-ordination with the other Swordfish.

A strong barrage came up at M2 but the shells were falling five hundred feet short. Shaw turned the Swordfish to starboard to avoid attacking from ahead, then at 2,000 feet turned to port and made his run in on the port beam, with tracer missing astern. At 800 yards he fired his first ripple of rockets, which fell short in line with the conning tower. At 500 yards he let go the second ripple, which went over.

G1 attacked almost simultaneously and caught more of the intense ack-ack fire than M2. As the Swordfish fired her full salvo of four rockets she was hit in the upper port mainplane and the engine by 20-millimetre shells. The oil and smoke which poured out prevented the crew from seeing the fall of shot.

Then G3 attacked. Cooper let go a half-ripple. They thought the R/P's had

*Ideally converted—***Rapana** *in harbour*

gone over and ahead but could not be sure owing to the violent avoiding action
which Cooper had to take in the face of the bursting shells. Then he fired his
second pair, which seemed to go over and hit the water forward of the conning
tower. The Swordfish turned sharply away to starboard and was hit in the
centre section by a 20-millimetre shell and in the port wing by 0.5-inch machine-
gun bullets, causing severe damage and inflating the dinghy which broke away
from the aircraft.

All three Swordfish reported damage. G1 dropped a marine marker to guide the escort ships which were speeding to the spot. While she was low above the water she was fired on again from the U-boat at a range of between 1,000 and 2,000 yards. Shells burst in pairs, straddling the wake of the aircraft between fifty and a hundred yards astern.

The two 'George' aircraft returned to the *Ancylus* safely. M2 continued to shadow the U-boat from two to three miles at about 3,000 feet. The submarine resumed her original course of 080°. She fired several rounds at the persistent Stringbag from her heavy gun, which made large splashes in the sea below, then, seven minutes after M2's attack had been made, submerged. M2 also returned safely to her carrier, and the convoy reached Halifax on June 1st.

Adula accompanied a convoy which left Gourock in May. Bad weather made flying impossible for *Adula*'s P-Flight of three Swordfish and restricted U-boat activity. But on the twelfth day out the weather moderated and the sky cleared. About midnight the SOE intercepted signals from a wolf pack which enabled him to fix their position about eighty miles south-west of the convoy. P-Flight were ordered to make a pre-dawn search of the area round the position. *Adula* dropped astern of the convoy, and at 0359 her Master, Captain Rumbellow, began his turn into wind. Twenty seconds later Lieutenant Godley, who commanded P-Flight, took off into the dark. They headed south at 1,500 feet.

They flew on over the empty ocean until they reached the U-boats' last known position, then split up to search the area. They covered the 4,000 square miles of sea in an hour and a half, sighting nothing, then turned for home. A few minutes later Godley suddenly sighted a large three-masted schooner ahead, rolling on the lonely sea with bare poles. He had not recovered from his astonishment when his observer, Lieutenant Jake Bennett, sighted another Swordfish away on their starboard beam at the limit of visibility, flying almost parallel to them. They were just thinking how remarkable it was that two aircraft should be returning exactly together after a long flight by dead reckoning, when, without warning, their engine failed.

Godley kept the Swordfish in the shallowest glide possible and tried to re-start the engine. As the machine glided silently down the TAG, Leading Airman Simpson, reported the radio dead. At 800 feet Godley fired the rocket projectiles to reduce the weight for ditching and to attract the schooner's attention, although she was only six or seven miles away and must have seen them.

The Swordfish sat down gently on the sea. The first thing Godley noticed was that the large inflatable rubber dinghy in the upper mainplane did not automatically inflate as it should have done, although there were always the three small individual dinghies, one attached to the pilot's parachute, the other two stowed in the after cockpits. Shrugging out of his parachute harness, Godley climbed out of his cockpit and tried to get the big dinghy to inflate with the emergency release. As he was doing this the Swordfish sank, taking with it the big dinghy and Godley's and Bennett's small ones.

In water four degrees above freezing the three men clung on, up to their armpits in the sea, to Simpson's tiny dinghy, and waited for the schooner to pick them up. What they did not know was that the ship had not seen them, or even heard the roar of their rockets, so intent had the fishermen been on their nets, which were out to the north, while the Swordfish approached them from the south.

But the crew of the other Swordfish had seen them. The pilot, Sub-Lieutenant Ian Parkin, immediately flew towards them, and his observer, Sub-Lieutenant Stanley Holness, flashed the schooner with his Aldis lamp.

The only reaction of the ship's captain was to spread out an outsize Red Ensign on the deck. Parkin gave up and flew over to the spot where Godley, Bennett and Simpson floated, diving again and again on their position, dropping flares and smoke-floats to attract the attention of the schooner.

There was a heavy swell running and the three men in the sea had lost sight of the schooner as soon as the Swordfish had hit the water. All they could do was hang desperately on to the little dinghy, with Bennett and Simpson being seasick and all of them feeling the deadly numbness creeping up their bodies. For Godley the effort of hanging on began to be too great. Life did not seem to be worth the effort. He said to Bennett, 'Jake, I don't think I can be bothered to hold on any longer.'

At that moment above the wave crests appeared the rolling tops of three masts. The meaning of Parkin's antics had at last got through to the schooner captain. He had had no sails set but had started his engine and come to investigate. They lowered a boat and began to row towards the airmen, who were now in a very bad way, having been immersed in the near-freezing sea for fifty minutes. When the boat came alongside them they lost consciousness.

Godley awoke to the sight of a swinging paraffin lamp and the sound of German voices. His first thought was that he was in a U-boat. But the fishermen of the *Kasagra* were from a German settlement at Lunenburg, Nova Scotia. They poured brandy down his throat and looked after the airmen with great care and attention until a corvette arrived from the convoy for them.

'Doc' Moffatt in the *Adula* had been very worried that the well-meaning fishermen would do the wrong thing—and try to *warm* the frozen men up. But they well understood the problems of exposure at sea, and kept the patients *cold*, with ice. This treatment was continued aboard the convoy's hospital ship, to which they were transferred. After two days of being packed round with hot water bottles filled with ice, some feeling returned to their limbs, to the extent that they could just feel a needle jabbed in half an inch, and they were reduced to being refrigerated only every other hour. After a week or two they could walk on crutches, although they were not fit to fly on the return trip. This convoy, with a hundred and twenty ships, was the largest ever to sail the Atlantic.

Empire MacColl escorted a convoy back to the United Kingdom in May. The convoy had reached a position about 500 miles from Ireland, and *Empire MacColl* was scheduled to supply two aircraft for the next dawn patrol, one to fly on the port beam, one on the starboard beam of the convoy.

Twice take-off was abandoned because of thick fog. At the first break in the weather after that the ASO, Lieutenant-Commander 'Tween' Neil, wanted the two aircraft to take off. Captain Goodchild objected that although the weather was fairly clear just then, fog had been lifting and dropping for some hours and might be a grave danger to the aircrews. But there had been greater U-boat activity than usual during the voyage, and Neil insisted that the patrol be flown.

There was barely any wind and to cut down on their weight the two Swordfish were readied with only half a tankful of petrol. Even so the weight of rockets, depth charges and the Mark II radar scanner all combined to increase the danger of stalling on take-off.

The batsman . . .

The two machines got safely into the air, but within two minutes the starboard aircraft reported itself in thick fog and requested permission to return to the ship. Permission was granted. The second Swordfish, piloted by Sub-Lieutenant W. G. 'Hank' Coates with Sub-Lieutenant Geoffrey Banks as observer and Leading Airman 'Taff' Roach as the telegraphist-air-gunner, hit the fog five minutes later. Their request to be allowed to return to the *Empire MacColl* was also granted, but when they reached the convoy it was completely obliterated by the fog.

They had no equipment for blind landings and could only hope for a gap in the fog. But the ship could not turn out of line indefinitely to receive them, and after half an hour's fruitless circling in the murk without even a glimpse of the carrier the TAG passed Banks the ominous signal 'Jettison all unnecessary load and set course for nearest land—TRACK 120°, DISTANCE 275 MILES.'

Banks did a quick calculation. To a Swordfish with less than half a tank of petrol and a groundspeed of 80 mph this meant, by all normal criteria, that they would have to ditch about seventy miles from land. He seized the chance of picking up a long cylindrical smoke-canister, which he had for months begged his armourer not to put in the cockpit as it always rolled about on the deck and got in his way, and heaved it over the side with a satisfied shout, then hoped that it would not brain anyone on the ships, which were still hidden below them in the fog.

The first hour passed, then the second, broken only by the TAG's periodic signals to *Empire MacColl* to report their position. They flew as low as possible so as to be able to see any friendly ships or sign of land, and expected to lose

. . . bringing in a Swordfish

touch with the ship after about a hundred miles, but to their surprise the TAG managed to remain in contact.

As ditching time approached they checked their survival drill and braced themselves. But the time came and the engine sputtered on. They began thinking, 'Fifty miles to go . . . forty . . . thirty . . .' Banks switched on the radar and was surprised to get a huge echo. He homed on it.

Coates shouted, 'There's a dirty great battleship ahead!' Two minutes later he amended this to, 'It's a dirty great rock that looks like a dirty great battleship in all this fog.' Soon more and more rocks were sighted, then solid land. At that point the main tank gave out and the pilot switched to the gravity tank.

They flew in thankfully over green fields. The pilot selected a field which looked smooth enough, though it was very small, with a wall down one side. He landed the Swordfish beautifully, though he had to brake sharply as the wall loomed. The Stringbag tipped gently forward, then sank back, quite intact, with only an inch of earth on each propellor blade tip to suggest anything out of the ordinary.

Without any land maps they had no idea where they were, whether in Ulster

After the gale: aboard Empire MacKay

Write-offs: the flight deck of **Empire MacKay**

or Eire. A harsh voice called out from behind them, 'Are youse English?' They spun round. A tall figure in ancient clothes was aiming a shotgun at them. By his side was an enormous Irish wolfhound. They were not sure whether admitting to English nationality was the best thing to do, but it seemed to be more acceptable than German as the man took them off to his home, a very humble place with a hole in the roof for a chimney and a peat fire burning. There was no food in the house, but he offered them goat's milk, all he had. He was dour but kindly, his only suggestion being 'Youse'll need to wait for the Military.'

The Military duly arrived, in the form of Commandant Paddy and his driver in a Ford V8 Pilot. Deeply suspicious, having dutifully learned and absorbed their Drill For Landing In A Neutral Country, the airmen insisted first on speaking to Their Man in Dublin, and second on leaving the TAG to guard the aircraft. The Commandant affably agreed to all their demands and drove them to the nearest telephone box. A very Whitehall voice said, 'Oh yes, you're the chaps who've just force-landed in County Mayo. Well, now, you are to do exactly as Commandant Paddy tells you. That's an order. *Good*-bye!'

The Commandant, grinning broadly, produced a bottle of Irish whisky and poured them two full tumblers. They poured them straight into very empty stomachs, and were driven back to the landing field, where Roach had folded the wings and put on the cockpit covers. Commandant Paddy then told them their fate, which would begin with a drive to the near-by town of Belmullet, eight miles away, where rooms had been booked for them in the hotel, followed by a hot bath, something to eat and a 'tour of the town'.

The whisky and the friendliness and the Consul's words made it seem more and more foolish, not to say boorish, to insist on the letter of the law. They did diffidently mention the necessity of standing guard over the aircraft in shifts. Commandant Paddy said, 'Ah, now, what would be the point of that? Aren't I after sending for a whole battalion of Irish Militia with tents and rifles and all —to do the job for you? Won't you let 'em? Sure, they don't get much opportunity.'

The Militia and the tents arrived and the airmen departed in the Ford V8 to the best hotel in Belmullet. On a dining-room table was the biggest salmon they had ever seen. They ate it all, and everything else produced for them.

This they had cause to regret, as the 'tour of the town', which began immediately afterwards, entailed a call at every house in every street for 'a sup and a bite'. It was a night of huge Irish hospitality. Taff Roach, a firm teetotaller, was reassured with 'Ah, now, it won't do you any harm. Sure, even the baby drinks it.'

A wild night was followed by a late awakening and a much later breakfast. Then, consciences painfully dictated a return in the V8 to the aircraft—against Commandant Paddy's assurances, who finally gave in 'as you are so concerned'. They found two civilians climbing all over the Swordfish, quite unhindered by the battalion of Militia. When challenged, one of them jumped down and with a languid smile announced that he was Flight Lieutenant Kite of the RAF and that the other man was his fitter. Under raincoats they both wore full RAF uniform. They had crossed the border from Ulster in a truck with sixty gallons of fuel. The fitter had thoroughly vetted the aircraft and found it airworthy. He had also found that a section of the fuel pipe had been wrongly connected aboard the *Empire MacColl*. But for this mistake, which had impeded the flow of petrol, they really would have had to ditch seventy miles from land.

While they talked, a soldier wireless-operator brought a message to the Commandant, who swiftly swept them into the V8 and the RAF men into their truck. The two vehicles drove off, and they were told that it had been fixed for them to take off after lunch, fly into Ulster, and land at RAF St. Angelo to be de-briefed. The escape was being handled exclusively by the Military. The civil authorities were kept, officially at least, in ignorance, but the Chief of Police, who was not friendly, was at that moment on his way to the aircraft, so they would have to choose their take-off time well.

At the hotel they ate a huge lunch, then returned to the field. The wind had changed. Landing had been remarkably easy, as the wind then had been blowing along the diagonal of the field. Now it blew from the side, the side of the stone wall and the main road. They would have an even shorter distance for take-off, the wall, telegraph wires and then trees. To make things worse, a lot of people appeared on the road to see them off. They had left their work in the only large building in the area, a toy factory, to see the fun.

At the last minute came a message that the Chief of Police's car, which had been misdirected several times on its way to the landing field, was now heading their way. There was no time for checks or good-byes.

They jumped in and were off, with a clear round over the obstacles. After a low farewell flight of thanks over the town, covering every street, where everyone came out to wave, they flew along the coast, using a map supplied by the Flight Lieutenant, and over County Sligo. To their great amusement the TAG picked up the *Empire MacColl*'s other two aircraft, which had just left the ship and were requesting permission to set course for Maydown, the ship having reached a position near the mouth of Lough Foyle. When Swordfish ABC1 and ABC2 had finished speaking, they chipped in with a brisk,

'Hello ABC from ABC3. Request permission to proceed to base.'

There was a long pause, then an incredulous 'SAY AGAIN.'

They landed at St. Angelo, were de-briefed by RAF Intelligence there, and left for Maydown.

In May one more tanker MAC-ship, the Anglo-Saxon Company's *Macoma*, went into service, the nineteenth of her kind and the last to commission. The situation had improved so much that the other thirteen planned were not converted. In June and July aircraft and crews were reduced by one in each MAC-ship and these diverted to the Naval squadrons involved in 'Overlord'. Lieutenant Godley's crew from *Adula* joined No. 816 Squadron, a unit with a fine record against U-boats, and patrolled the Channel uneventfully for several weeks until re-called to 836, when Godley joined *Adula* again.

Against the Normandy invasion the Germans introduced a new submarine device, the *schnorkel*, copied from a captured Dutch submarine. This was a long breathing pipe which could be extended to project above the surface of the sea, so that a U-boat could run submerged on her diesels, which gave her a fast passage to and from her operational area, with immunity from aircraft. Armed with the schnorkel, German submarines became a serious menace once more.

A patrolling Swordfish would dive on anything suspicious, and in bad visibility it was easy to make mistakes. One aircraft fired her whole broadside of eight rocket projectiles at a large fish. The same aircraft was returning to her carrier at the end of a patrol when the visibility, which had been about four miles, suddenly closed down to a few hundred yards. In a gap through the mist the observer saw a white wake below and a blurred shape. The Swordfish dived at once, the pilot's hand on the firing switch—and pulled up just in time to avoid the superstructure of the *Aquitania*.

On June 11th *Empire MacMahon*, *Empire MacCabe* and *Miralda* sailed with convoy ON240, a big convoy of eighty-six merchantmen. On the 21st in response to a signal from SOE, two Swordfish from *Miralda* and one from *Empire MacCabe* were flown off at 1530. After eighty minutes' flying, at 1705, the pilot of one machine, Lieutenant H. P. Dawson, saw a wake below and ahead. The weather was bad, the visibility poor. He dived to investigate and asked his observer, Sub-Lieutenant Jones, to check that it was not a whale.

There was a dark brown shape in the water, with a vertical lump amidships. Dawson dropped a marker and circled back, but the wake had gone and there was no oil slick or air bubbles. Jones and Leading Airman Brotherhood, the TAG, both thought that they had seen a surfacing U-boat, but the more experienced Dawson felt sure it was a whale. Another Swordfish, eighty miles from the convoy, sighted a suspected submerged U-boat at 1745, which had dived before they could attack it. Another aircraft was flown off as a strike, but saw nothing. Between them the three carriers kept one aircraft over the area until dark. Several whales were reported, and one object much larger, which had broken surface, then dived again. This was recorded as a whale also.

The whole of this search was flown in very bad weather, and two of *Miralda's* Swordfish were damaged in landing-on, but were repaired on board. On June 29th, when ONS242 was three days out of the Clyde, an aircraft from *Macoma* smashed its undercarriage beyond repair on landing. To make use of the redundant crew, *Rapana* flew her spare Swordfish to *Macoma*.

The restricted space of the MAC-ships' flight decks was an inducement to accidents, though the skill of the handling parties usually kept these to a minimum. Rough weather tested their efforts severely, adding frequent hazards to take-off and landing and spotting the deck, and making maintenance a grinding chore, especially in the tanker conversions with no hangars, in which all servicing had to be done on the open flight deck, which might be pitching and rolling badly and taking green seas aboard.

All through one brilliant summer day when *Empire MacAlpine* was returning home with a convoy, the surface escorts had been away out of sight, apparently fighting an action with U-boats, leaving the convoy without protection. There were no clouds in the sky, and there was no wind, so the Swordfish could not take off with depth charges or rockets. Night came and the escorts had still not returned. Buzzes flew round the ship . . . There were at least sixty U-boats in the vicinity . . . The escorts had been decoyed away, leaving the ships of the convoy sitting ducks for the wolf packs which lay in wait ahead of them . . . All through that long night the aircrews sat, in their flying kit, in the Ready Room, talking, singing, drinking coffee, inwardly more frightened than they had ever been. Only when the dawn came with no attacks, and the escorts returned, could they relax.

Stern view of **Rapana** *showing the 4-inch gun and wind-breakers on the flight deck*

The *Ancylus* left Halifax with convoy HX299 on July 13th, 1944, for a non-operational voyage with a cargo of eight naval aircraft on the flight deck, but on the 15th developed engine trouble and had to drop astern of the convoy. Repairs were completed in an anxious two hours, twenty-eight minutes, but the ship was ordered to St. Johns to wait for the next convoy, HX300.

At St. Johns the YMCA organised a concert on the flight deck, followed by a dance, held between decks owing to rain. The Captain provided rum punch, and the Chief Steward and his staff impressed everyone with their high-class buffet. There was deck-hockey and several games of football were played ashore. There were the usual contributions from Service and Merchant Navy 'Comforts' organisations, games and records from the Canadian Red Cross, which also gave the ship a duplicator to print the ship's newspaper, 'Ancylus Herald', which had been started at the beginning of the voyage.

HX300 left Halifax on July 19th. One Swordfish on patrol from another MAC-ship in the convoy sent a distress signal from a position about seventy miles from the convoy. HF/DF bearings on the aircraft were established by SOE and the rescue ship *Zamalek*. The Swordfish switched her IFF to the distress signal, which was picked up by radar types 272 and 242 at sixty miles. Bearings and ranges were passed to the aircraft's observer to help him check their position, and the aircraft closest to them on the search was sent to their assistance. This machine was homed to the distressed Swordfish from a range of forty-five miles. Both aircraft returned in company using radar type 251M as a check on navigation.

Flying routine in a convoy was now normally organised on the basis of two MAC-ships working as a unit. Flying took the form of searches, mainly ahead, to a depth of from sixty-five to seventy miles, each MAC-ship taking a twelve-hour tour of duty unless her aircraft flew a strike, in which case the MAC next for duty became duty MAC from the time of landing-on of the flying MAC's aircraft, for the next twelve hours.

At a meeting before ONF252 sailed it was agreed to fly routine daily searches ahead or in the most likely direction with three aircraft at dusk and dawn to a depth of eighty miles. On interception of a HF/DF signal nearby two aircraft would be automatically flown off without further orders. If an aircraft sighted an enemy all available aircraft from both carriers would be flown off as a strike. General routine was for the duty carrier to fly dawn and dusk searches, with the non-duty carrier standing by to provide a strike if called for while they were in the air. Carriers would change duty every flying day.

The two MAC's in ONF252 were *Empire MacAlpine* and *Miralda*. One of *Miralda*'s Swordfish damaged the tailplane of another while running up. A spare tailplane was transferred from *Empire MacAlpine*, which was a grain ship, with a hangar and more spares and facilities than the tanker, to an escort vessel, which passed it over to *Miralda*. As the ship did not carry equipment for testing the shock loading of engines, the repaired machine was not flown on routine patrols but held in reserve. Water made all the aircraft R/T sets unserviceable during a heavy rainstorm. It took twenty-four hours to repair two of the sets, and the third was not fixed until the aircraft had flown off to Dartmouth when the convoy reached Canadian waters. Canvas covers were made and there was no further trouble.

Gales did serious damage to *Empire MacKay*'s aircraft during one outward voyage, and she entered Halifax with her flight deck looking like a Swordfish graveyard. A crippled aircraft was a particular nuisance to a tanker MAC-ship. With no hangar in which to stow it, the damaged machine had to be spotted right aft while the other Swordfish took off, which cut down their run, and manhandled up to the bows again for each landing-on. If a Swordfish crashed badly on the flight deck and was damaged beyond the capacity of the ship to repair her, she was usually dumped overboard. Sometimes, after any valuable instruments had been removed, the ship's crew would be given a short time in which to collect souvenirs from the aircraft. In such cases the whole aircraft invariably disappeared. Swordfish, at this stage of the war, were expendable.

If a Swordfish crew became redundant on a homeward voyage, due to a crash, life became difficult for them when the ship reached home waters. Instead of flying off straight from the ship to Maydown, the unfortunate airmen had to stay in the ship until she docked in the Clyde, then struggle back, with all their kit, which normally filled their cockpits, by train and ferry to Northern Ireland.

Miralda returned home with convoy HXF310, which sailed through the centre of a tropical storm. The wind went right off the anemometer, which registered up to 60 knots, maintained a steady 70 for hours on end, and at times gusted to 90 knots. Green seas struck *Miralda*'s starboard quarter and swept aft. But the Swordfish had been well lashed down with one hundred and twenty fathoms of one-and-a-half-inch rope to every possible securing point, in addition to the normal wire lashings. It was taken for granted that the controls and fuselages would have been strained, but all were found afterwards to be in good shape.

Patrolling Swordfish still got into difficulties with their navigation. Swordfish D2, pilot Lieutenant Frame, observer Sub-Lieutenant Owen, from *Empire MacAlpine* missed the convoy, ON272, returning in rain and cloud on December 14th, 1944, and requested a homing. Their IFF was not visible on the ship's radar, so the aircraft was ordered to orbit and transmit on radio so that they could be homed by HF/DF. *Empire MacAlpine* converted their first bearing into a magnetic course to steer and passed it to them, but just then their IFF distress signals were picked up on radar, which took over the job and brought the wanderer home.

What Swordfish crews hated most was a patrol astern of the convoy, and no ASO liked ordering one. Overtaking a convoy for a slow aircraft like the Swordfish could be a grim struggle. To an aircraft sixty miles behind the convoy a sudden change of wind could bring disaster. During one voyage when two MAC-ships were in company, a Swordfish returning to her parent carrier was heading back towards the convoy from astern when the wind suddenly veered and blew from ahead at about 60 knots, reducing the Swordfish's actual speed

Still life: Empire MacAndrew *and seagulls*

to about 20 knots. Radar operators in the MAC-ship watched the tiny blip on their screens until, with petrol exhausted, it faded out. The Swordfish was never seen again.

The schnorkel U-boats were having some success. They sank 59,000 tons in December 1944 with few losses themselves. The brunt of U-boat hunting was borne by the escort groups, which included escort carriers, but MAC Swordfish made some contacts. At 0827 on the morning of December 27th Swordfish M3H from *Miralda* reported an oil slick fifteen miles from her convoy, ON274, which made an emergency turn to starboard to pass outside the torpedo danger zone. Bubbles, then a periscope followed, and M3H, pilot Sub-Lieutenant Parkin, observer Sub-Lieutenant Holness, TAG Leading Airman Hawkins, attacked. A good straddle spaced at thirty-five feet was scored with two 100-pound anti-submarine bombs set for eighteen feet. A box search of the area failed to re-establish contact. On January 18th, 1945, *Empire MacCabe* recorded a possible sighting, which did not develop.

There was a combat between a schnorkel U-boat and a MAC-ship on April 12th, 1945. Convoy ON296, with MAC-ships *Empire MacAlpine* and *Adula*, left the Clyde on the 11th. At 1500 on the 12th a ship was hit by a torpedo about thirty-five miles away from the convoy, on a bearing 152° in position 53°48′ North, 04°49′ West.

At 1522 a Swordfish from *Empire MacAlpine*'s Y Flight of 836 Squadron, commanded by Lieutenant K. C. Price, took off armed with two depth-charges, saw the torpedoed ship, a Liberty ship, which was down by the head and making about seven knots, but returned at 1715 without having seen any U-boats. At 1810 the pilot of another aircraft, which had been flown off at 1615, saw a schnorkel, which his ASV radar did not pick up, break surface just below his port wing when the Swordfish was at 200 feet. He attacked at once but the schnorkel disappeared while the Swordfish was turning. He dropped his two depth-charges, set for sixteen feet, sixty feet ahead of the point where the schnorkel had disappeared. At 1825 this aircraft was recalled and another armed with two depth-charges flown off to replace it, but neither this crew nor the next, which flew off at 1930, made any further contact. Then at 2020 it looked as if the escorts on the port side of the convoy had found something, as the black pendant was being flown and gunfire could be seen and heard from that direction. *Empire MacAlpine*'s ASO asked SO Escort if the Swordfish could be of any use, and was told that the situation was 'well in hand'. Shortly afterwards *U-1024* surfaced and surrendered; she was manned by a boarding party and towed into harbour.

On April 20th a Swordfish from *Empire MacAndrew*, sailing in convoy ON298, sighted a periscope and dropped two depth-charges on it, but with no visible result. This was the last contact between a Merchant Aircraft Carrier and a U-boat.

On May 21st, 1945, No. 836 Squadron was disbanded, being the last operational squadron to fly Swordfish. This unique and remarkable unit was by far the largest squadron in the Fleet Air Arm. As each new MAC-ship drew near completion, a new flight of three or four Swordfish was formed at Maydown. Each flight was given a letter of the alphabet. The allocation got as far as 'S'— nineteen flights in all, or sixty-three aircrews. There was always a very fine spirit in the Squadron, due in no small part to the founder, Lieutenant-Commander Slater, and owing much to the very positively defined identity of the unit and its role.

Empire MacColl

On June 28th, 1945, the MAC-ship service came to an end with the arrival in Britain of the *Empire MacKay*. The flight of a Swordfish from her deck on the 27th was actually the last operational flight of a Swordfish in the history of the Fleet Air Arm.

Merchant Aircraft Carriers had made in all one hundred and seventy round trips with Atlantic convoys, a total of 4,447 days at sea, including 3,057 spent in convoy. Flying took place on 1,183 of these days, during which the Merchant Swordfish put in 9,016 flying hours on 4,177 sorties.

Their role was to provide aircraft to keep the U-boats off the merchantmen, to look after the convoys so that the escort carriers, their stronger-muscled sisters, could use their full potential as small Fleet carriers, a role which they filled very successfully as U-boat hunters with the Support Groups, in attacks against German ships and shore bases in Norway, with Admiral Vian's big carriers at Salerno, and against the Japanese in support of the army in Burma. MAC-ships were economical, as well as effective substitutes for escort carriers with the convoys. A MAC-ship took an average of five months to convert from a merchantman, about a third of the time taken to build an escort carrier on a merchant hull, at a fraction of the cost.

It was a particularly satisfying thing that the merchant ships should be given aircraft which they could regard as their own, which they took to sea with them and which could not be taken from them for some unknown purpose, as their Royal Navy escorts so frequently were. The Merchant Stringbags, like the CAM-Hurricanes before them, were really a refined form of the guns which had been given to the merchantmen under the Defensively Equipped Merchant Ships scheme, and their crews filled a similar role to the Navy DEMS gunners. They greatly boosted the morale of every convoy in which they sailed.

The Merchant Navy regarded them as its own. For their part, Temporary, ex-civilian, RNVR airmen often found it particularly fitting that they should have been given the job of protecting the sea-going civilians who were going about the unwarlike, life-giving task of feeding the nation. It was so vividly symbolic of the basic role of an armed navy. The fact that they themselves brought home each trip, in their own improvised ships of war, 10,000 tons of grain or oil, made it even more satisfying.

The faith of the merchant seamen in their merchant aircraft was well justified. Out of two hundred and seventeen convoys in which Merchant Aircraft Carriers were included only one was successfully attacked by U-boats. The merchant Swordfish kept a lot of heads down, and in addition co-operated with the surface escorts in several U-boat kills or captures. These were the sort of statistics that made sense to the weary, nerve-racked survivors of the Battle of the Atlantic. If there was a MAC-ship in the convoy, they slept the better for it.

With the end of the war the MAC-ships, like their RNVR aircrews, were demobbed. Flight decks, hangars, guns, were removed. Captains found they had room to breathe in again after two years spent imprisoned in a small steel cell, conning an airfield across the Atlantic. The huge and smiling relief of sailing a sea without U-boats under a sky clear forever of Focke-Wulfs swamped the occasional pang of nostalgia for the revving of Pegasus engines, the unfailing, morbid fascination of landing-on. The MAC-ships shed their uniforms of grey and put on their brighter civvy suits.

Empire MacColl became an orthodox tanker once again and was re-named *British Pilot*. Her voyages took her mostly to the Persian Gulf. Captain Goodchild remained in command of her until the end of 1946, when he went to Birkenhead to take command of a new ship, the *British Baron*, a 12,412 tons deadweight tanker, which was completed in February, 1947. This ship was withdrawn from service by the end of 1959, at which time the former MAC-ship was still making voyages to Iran.

In the decade 1953–63 all nine of the Anglo-Saxon Petroleum ex-MAC-ships were scrapped. They had all been built in the early thirties and had come naturally to the end of an exceptionally useful life. The *Iacra*, ex-*Acavus*, was the last of these to go, in an Italian breaker's yard. Of the British Petroleum MAC-ships, the *Empire MacKay* was scrapped at Rotterdam in 1960, *Empire MacMahon*, by then *Navinia*, scrapped in Hong Kong in the same year, *Empire MacCabe* at Hong Kong in 1962.

In 1957 Captain Goodchild retired from the sea and went to live near Poole, in Dorset, close to the sea and ships. In the summer of 1962 he went on holiday in Scotland. One day he was driving along the side of Gare Loch, when he passed a shipbreaker's yard. A ship in the early stages of being broken up seemed familiar to him. He stopped and got out of the car to take a closer look. There, under the swinging iron ball and the hissing blue torches, was his old *British Pilot*, ex-*Empire MacColl*.

Saddened, Captain Goodchild got back into the car. For the next few minutes he forgot about the glowing Scottish landscape which lay around him . . . Ahead in the half light of dawn was a great spread of ships as the MAC-ship dropped slowly astern of the convoy . . . He gave a brisk helm order, and the

Peace again: Macoma *in her normal role*

big grey slab of the deck swung ponderously round into wind . . . From aft there was the throbbing racket of a Pegasus engine at full revs . . . The noise swelled and surged past him and a white Swordfish rose from the wet, heaving deck . . . One of the three young men hunched in the cockpits waved a hand nonchalantly . . .

For a second Captain Goodchild almost waved back. Then he remembered where he was. He raised his hand, switched on the engine, and drove away. The sun came out as he drove along the Loch. He forgot about the breaker's yard and began to enjoy his holiday once more.

Of the grain-carriers, the *Empire MacCallum*, after thirteen years of general trading under Greek management, bearing the pseudonyms of *Doris Clunies*, *Sunrover*, *Eudoxia* and *Phorkyss*, was broken up at Osaka, Japan in 1960.

The other five are, at the time of writing, still afloat. Four of them can be seen tramping the ports of the world, from Cardiff to Yokahama.

The *Empire MacKendrick* became the *Granpond* in 1947, under Greek management, and in 1951 the *Condor*. In 1957 she joined the Turnbull Scott Shipping Company of London, and was re-christened *Saltersgate*, then in 1959 was sold across the Iron Curtain to Navigation Maritime Bulgare as the *Vassil Levsky*, registered at Varna. In June, 1967, *Vassil Levsky* had begun a northbound passage through the Suez Canal system when the Six Day War began between Israel and the United Arab Republic. Soon after hostilities began the Egyptians blocked the Canal. Fourteen merchant ships were trapped in the Bitter Lakes, and are there still, at the time of writing, including the *Vassil Levsky*, which dropped anchor on June 6th.

Empire MacAlpine and *Empire MacAndrew* both began their peacetime trading in British hands, as the *Derrynane* and *Derryheen* of McCowen and Gross Limited of Glasgow. In 1964 *Derryheen* became the *Patricia* of the Pomos Shipping Company, registered at Famagusta, Cyprus, and was last reported leaving Porto Alegre in southern Brazil for Trieste.

Empire MacRae and *Empire MacDermott* have both traded extensively for Greek owners. The *MacRae* is, at the time of writing, the tramp *Despina P.*, sailing somewhere between Gdynia and Rotterdam. In 1948 she joined the

Twenty years on . . .
Top: Suva Breeze (*ex*-Empire MacAlpine) *in 1965*
Centre: Tobon (*ex*-Empire MacRae) *in 1967*
Bottom: Vassil Levsky (*ex*-Empire MacKendrick) *in 1970*

Alpha South African Steamship Company as the *Alpha Zambesi*. In 1954 she became the *Tobon* under Norwegian owners and was seen at Cardiff Docks unloading grain. As the *Despina P.* she now belongs to the Aghiaparaskevi Corporation and is registered at Piraeus. *Empire MacDermott* became the *La Cumbre* of Buries Markes Limited in 1949, then the *Parnon*, registered at Piraeus, of the Canero Compania Noviera, in 1959. Ten years later she joined the Southern Shipping and Enterprises Company, and as the *Starlight*, registered at Mogadishu and flying the flag of convenience of the Somali Republic, tramps the Far East for cargoes from her base at Hong Kong.

Also ranging Far Eastern waters is the *Pacific Endeavour*, which, as the *Empire MacAlpine*, was the first MAC-ship, and the one to see most action. Starting peacetime trading as the *Derrynane*, in 1951 she became the *Huntsbrook* of the Power Steamship Navigation Company of London, which she remained until 1959 when she was acquired by the South Breeze Navigation Company under the management of the well-known Hong Kong firm of John Manners. Under various names she has continued to trade from Hong Kong under the same management. For a year she was the *Djatingaleh* and under charter to the Republic of Indonesia. A spell as the *San Ernesto* of the San Fernando Steamship Company followed, until she was given her present name of *Pacific Endeavour* in 1968. As she leaves Singapore Roads for Nagoya, it is difficult to see her as the grey aircraft carrier on the flat deck of which Lieutenant Commander Slater landed the first Merchant Swordfish over a quarter of a century ago.

MERCHANT AIRCRAFT CARRIERS—General Details

GRAIN CARRIERS

Empire MacAlpine, Empire MacKendrick

Converted by Burntisland Shipbuilding Company.

Displacement:	7,950 tons.
Dimensions:	Length $433\frac{3}{4}$ feet (over all). Beam $56\frac{3}{4}$ feet. Draught $24\frac{1}{2}$ feet. Flight deck $413\frac{3}{4} \times 62$ feet.
Machinery:	1 shaft Diesel motor. BHP 3,300.
Max. Speed:	$12\frac{1}{2}$ knots.
Armament:	1 4-inch, 2 40-millimetre AA, 4 20-millimetre guns. 4 aircraft.
Complement:	107.

Empire MacAndrew, Empire MacDermott

Converted by Denny Brothers Ltd.

Displacement:	7,950 tons.
Dimensions:	Length $445\frac{3}{4}$ feet. Beam 56 feet. Draught $24\frac{3}{4}$ feet. Flight deck 423×62 feet.

Machinery, max. speed, armament and complement as for *Empire MacAlpine* class.

Empire MacRae, Empire MacCallum

Converted by Lithgows Ltd.

Displacement:	8,250 tons.
Dimensions:	Length $444\frac{1}{2}$ feet (over all). Beam $57\frac{3}{4}$ feet. Draught $24\frac{1}{2}$ feet. Flight deck $424\frac{1}{2} \times 62$ feet.

Machinery, max. speed, armament and complement as for *Empire MacAlpine* class.

OIL TANKERS

British Petroleum Company

Empire MacKay

Converted by Harland & Wolff (Govan) Co., Ltd.

Displacement:	8,908 tons.
Dimensions:	Length $482\frac{3}{4}$ feet (over all). Beam 59 feet. Draught $27\frac{1}{2}$ feet. Flight deck 460×62 feet.
Machinery:	1 shaft Diesel motor. BHP 3,300.
Max. Speed:	11 knots.
Armament:	1 4-inch, 8 20-millimetre AA guns. 3 aircraft.
Complement:	110.

Empire MacColl

Converted by Cammel Laird Ltd.

Displacement:	9,133 tons.
Dimensions:	Length $481\frac{1}{2}$ feet (over all). Beam $61\frac{3}{4}$ feet. Draught $27\frac{3}{4}$ feet. Flight deck 461×62 feet.

Machinery, max. speed, armament and complement as for *Empire MacKay*.

Empire MacMahon
Converted by Swan Hunter: Hawthorn Leslie Ltd.
  Displacement: 8,856 tons.
  Dimensions: Length 483 feet (over all). Beam 59 feet.
                  Draught 27½ feet. Flight deck 461½ × 62 feet.
  Machinery, max. speed, armament and complement as for *Empire MacKay*.

Empire MacCabe
Converted by Swan Hunter: Hawthorn Leslie Ltd.
  Displacement: 9,249 tons.
  Dimensions: Length 485¾ feet (over all). Beam 61¼ feet.
                  Draught 27½ feet. Flight deck 461 × 62 feet.
  Machinery, max. speed, armament and complement as for *Empire MacKay*.

Anglo Saxon Petroleum Company

Acavus, Adula, Alexia, Amastra, Ancylus, Gadila, Macoma, Miralda, Rapana

  Displacement: 8,000 tons.
  Dimensions: Length 481 feet (*Acavus, Adula, Amastra, Ancylus* 482¼ feet).
                  Beam 59 feet.
                  Draught 27½ feet. Flight deck 461¾ × 62 feet.
  Machinery: 1 shaft Diesel motor. BHP 4,000.
                  (*Acavus, Adula, Amastra, Ancylus* 3,500).
  Max. Speed: 13 knots.
  Armament: 1 4-inch, 8 20-millimetre guns. 3 aircraft.

Analysis of MAC-ship Operations 1943, 1944, 1945

Year	No. of MAC-ships arriving in		No. of days at sea		No. of air sorties		No. of flying hours		Average flying hours/ ship/ passage	No. of days in convoy		No. of days flying took place		% of flying days to days in convoy	Aircraft lost or damaged beyond repair on board	Air personnel lost
	North America	UK	Out	In	Out	In	Out	In	Total	Out	In	Out	In	Out/In	Out/In	Out/In
1943	14	13	207	171	159	123	332	235	21	178	171	not known	not known		19	1 aircrew
1944	116	100	1,643	1,295	1,452	1,151	3,189	2,437	26	971	777	436	327	44	74	4 crews, 2 leading airmen
1945 (6 mths)	40	40	605	526	742	550	1,660	1,163	35	487	473	233	187	44	21	1 pilot
Gross Totals	170	153	2,455	1,992	2,353	1,824	5,181	3,835	27 (mean average)	1,636	1,421	669	514	44	114*	
	323		4,447		4,177		9,016			3,057		1,183				

* 1 per 80 Operational Flying Hours

INDEX